Royal Families and Palaces of Gujarat

by Dr Hansdev Patel

SCORPION

CAVENDISH

LONDON

Cover:
WOOD CARVING, HALWAD PALACE, DHRANGADHRA;
(INSET) **NAULAKHA PALACE, GONDAL;**
(INSET) **NOOR BAKHTE BEGUM OF JUNAGADH, IN
TRADITIONAL NAWABI PERIOD ATTIRE, ON THE DAY
OF HER WEDDING TO SAHEB ZADA JABARDAST
KHAN OF PALANPUR**

Above:
**NAULAKHA PALACE, GONDAL WITH HIGHLY
ORNATE 17TH CENTURY AD SCULPTURED
STONE FACADE IN THE TYPICAL GUJARATI
STYLE**

First Published 1998
Second Edition 1999

ISBN 1 900269 20 1 (Softback Edition)

Scorpion Cavendish Ltd
31 Museum Street London WC1A 1LH England

Design: Adrian Knowles and Kathi Huidobro

Editor: Robert Rowe
Photographer: Dinesh Shukla, India

Printed and bound in England:
Lawrence-Allen Ltd, Weston-super-Mare

Contents

Dedication

To the great rulers of India – one of the world's least appreciated communities; to the royal families of Gujarat; and to Gujaratis all over the world, this book is respectfully dedicated.

Acknowledgments

In India I wish to thank Anil Mulchandani, the historian and travel consultant, without whom this project would not have been possible; Mahendra Mistry for watercolours; Jyoti Mulchandani and Kirti Shukla; and a special thank you to Dinesh Shukla for the excellent photographs taken especially for this book.

For providing accommodation, I would like to thank the Balaram Palace Resort in Palanpur; the Riverside Palace Hotel in Gondal; the GL Sharma Resort Hotel in Kutch; the Vijayraj Palace Hotel in Rajpipla; the Royal Oasis Hotel in Wankaner; the Nilambagh Palace and Palace Utelia Hotel in Bhavnagar; the Garden Palace in Balasinore; and the Kusum Vilas Palace in Chotta Udaipur.

For permission to photograph their properties, and for their kind hospitality, I would like to thank Rajmata Brijraj Nandini, HH Maharajah Vijayraj Sinhji and Shiv Badhra Sinhji of Bhavnagar; HH Maharajah Jyotendar Sinhji and Maharani Kumud Kumari of Gondal; Rajmata and Darbar Saheb Satyajit Kumar Khaccher of Jasdan; Dilip Sinhji and Gopal Sinhji Desai of Patdi; Raviraj Sinhji of the Shiv Mahal Palace, and Chandar Bjlani, V M Pandey, K M Thomas and Sharad Saxena and the staff of the Lalbagh Palace Railway Staff College, both in Baroda; HH Maharajah Raghuvir Sinhji, Maharani Rukmani Devi and Yuvraj Manvendar Sinhji of the Vijay Palace, and Rani Hemlata Devi of the Natwar Niwas Palace, both in Rajpipla; Maharani Vijaykuverba of Morvi; Thakore Saheb Chatrashailya Sinh of Limbdi; HH Maharajah Pratap Sinh and Yuvraj Dr Digvijay Sinh of Wankaner; HH Maharajah Virendra Sinhji, his son and daughter-in-law of Chotta Udaipur; the royal families of Dhrangadhra, Jamnagar and Junagadh; HH Maharao Pragmalji Prithviraj Sinh of the Ranjit Vilas Palace in Kutch; Nawab Muhammad Salabat Khan Babi and Begum Farhat Sultana of Balasinore; Nawab Saheb Iqbal Muhammad Khan Lohani of Palanpur, and Dilip Thakker of the Balaram Palace in Palanpur; HH Maharajah Chaitanya Dev Sinhji of the Rajmahal Palace in Wadhwan; and Yuvraj Mandatta Sinh of Rajkot.

For their valuable support in the research for this book, I wish to thank Sharad Vyas and Abhijit Vyas in Jamnagar; Bharat Rughani and Kishore Joshi in Porbandar; Khoram Khan in Palanpur and Pappu Soneja in Bhuj; and for providing useful background on the Heritage Hotels Association, I must thank Rao Gopal Sinh in Poshina.

In England I would like thank the publishers, Scorpion Cavendish Limited, Adrian Knowles and Richard Box; the editor Robert Rowe; the designer Kathi Huidobro; Walton Eddlestone; and Harendra de Silva QC of Porbandar and London. Thanks, too, to Paresh Desai and Pushant Patel for their introductions; to Dr L M Singhvi, former High Commissioner, and the High Commissioner, Shri Lallit Mansingh; and to Professor Indra Nath Choudhuri, Director of the Nehru Centre, London. Thanks also to Mahesh Lakhanpal and Manas Ranjan Pattanaik of the India Tourist Office, and to the staff at the British Library Oriental and India Office Collections, both in London.

Special thanks are due to my wife, Paru Patel, and to my friend, Brian Thatcher, for their unfailing encouragement and support.

The histories of the princely states tended to be told and re-told by the bards, and so inevitably there are a number of discrepancies and contradictions about various events, battles etc. I have tried to keep the book non-controversial, and, where these may occur, have attempted to recount the most acceptable story.

Foreword

This foreword is written not by an expert, but by someone who has had a fascination with India and Indian culture since an early age. Perhaps this is attributable to the fact that my father and his brothers and sisters were born in Coonoor, educated in Bangalore, and lived in the Nilgiri Hills district, Southern India. Indeed my forebears were reputed to have settled in India at the time of Clive. For someone intensely interested in history and my antecedents, it is frustrating that our family Bible went missing in the 1930s, and with it the details necessary to trace my ancestors in India. I do have a ceremonial sword belonging to a distant cousin – one Lieutenant Fahey of the Indian Army – but that's all!

Over twenty years ago, with my own afternoon programme on television, I interviewed an artist, John Nankivell, who had a particular affinity for the wonderful and varied architecture of India. He was a friend of Sir John Betjeman and his wife and accompanied Lady Betjeman on at least one of her Indian tours. The detail in his sketches and drawings has to be seen to be believed – the fine tracery on so many buildings looks just like lace. Another artist

friend, Andrew Hewkin, recently spent some months in the Himalayas where he sketched, photographed and painted. Two of his watercolours hang in my home.

I decided aeons ago that one day a lengthy holiday in India would be on the agenda – off the beaten track and away from the obvious tourist spots. But where. . . . ! India is such a vast country with so many different cultures – where does one start?

Dr Hansdev Patel has finally settled the question for me. In his fascinating, informative and highly readable book, Hans takes his reader on a magic carpet ride around fabulous, and beautifully photographed, architecture as he unfolds the history and the royal characters – with their amazing excesses, good works and style – who comprised in the past and today make up the princely states of Gujarat. Like our own aristocracy, many of the Gujarati royal families find it well nigh impossible to manage the financial upkeep of their palaces. Here in Britain large numbers of the great ancestral houses have been bequeathed to the National Trust, with the families retaining a wing for their own use. In Gujarat, many of the palaces are now open to tourists as Heritage Hotels, museums or monuments. What would your choice be: a stay in a cloned five-star hotel similar in design and service the world over – or the individuality and the magic of a palace echoing with history and romance?

Thank you Dr Hansdev Patel for the painstaking research undertaken to introduce your reader to the hitherto little known royal families and palaces of Gujarat.

Jan Leeming
Writer and Broadcaster

The Princely States of Gujarat

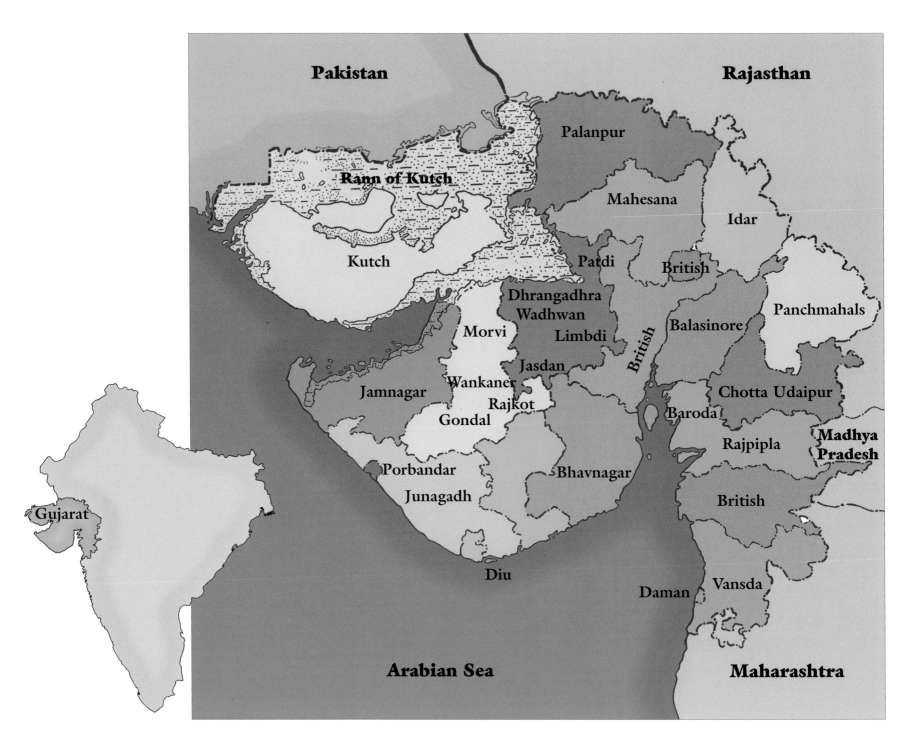

Pakistan

Rajasthan

Palanpur

Rann of Kutch

Mahesana

Idar

Kutch

Patdi

British

Dhrangadhra
Wadhwan

Panchmahals

Morvi

Limbdi

Balasinore

British

Jasdan

Wankaner

Chotta Udaipur

Jamnagar

Rajkot

Baroda

Gondal

Rajpipla

Madhya
Pradesh

Porbandar

Bhavnagar

British

Junagadh

Gujarat

Diu

Vansda

Daman

Arabian Sea

Maharashtra

Introduction

Few areas of the world are more evocative than the Indian subcontinent, with its exotic natural beauty and extraordinary contrasts. The princely rulers of India, with their opulent palaces and extravagant lifestyles, have been a source of fascination for centuries. Providence, it would seem, had created them with the sole intention of offering mankind a spectacle, a dazzling vision of marble palaces, tigers, elephants and jewels.

Before India's Independence in 1947AD, the 565 maharajahs, rajas, maharaos, maharanas, nawabs, thakore sahebs and other rulers held sway as absolute, hereditary sovereigns over one third of India's land surface and a quarter of her population. Many of the ruling dynasties had been in power, uninterrupted, for hundreds of years, and one particular dynasty can be traced back at least 2,000 years. They reflected the fact that, under the British, there had been two Indias: the India of the provinces, administered by the central government in Delhi, and a separate India with her 565 princely rulers. The anachronistic situation of the latter dated to Britain's haphazard conquest of India, when rulers who received the British with open arms, or who proved worthy foes on the battlefield, were allowed to remain on their thrones, provided that they acknowledged Britain as the paramount power in India. The rulers had absolute power over their subjects and – if they chose to (though only a handful did so) – could get away with almost any

NOOR BAKHTE BEGUM OF JUNAGADH, OF THE BABI DYNASTY, MARRIED TO SAHEB ZADA JABARDAST KHAN OF PALANPUR'S LOHANI DYNASTY, GRANDMOTHER OF THE PRESENT BEGUM OF BALASINORE

kind of outrageous behaviour without the British disturbing them – provided that their loyalty remained intact. The British had applied most effectively the doctrine of "Divide and Rule", and it was then a matter of ruling the rulers.

The term "princely states" is a misnomer. These states were not ruled by "princes" but by "kings", some of whom enjoyed a truly ancient heritage of political power. British Imperial ideology meant, however, that there was only the one "king" or "queen", and the Indian rulers were, and had to be, "princes". These martial families, whose forebears had lived exclusively for war, had borne sons whose aspirations had been to equip their armies with the most modern weapons and to wage endless war on their rivals. Under the British, their sons' ambitions were reduced to increasing the number of guns in their salute, to equipping their garages with the most up-to-date machinery from Mercedes, Rolls Royce and American manufacturers, and to reducing the wildlife population of the world by collecting trophies for their palaces.

The size and wealth of the states, over which the princes had total autonomy, varied greatly. A good

Introduction

HH Maharajah Vijay Sinhji of Rajpipla, on a tiger shoot, 1935AD

HH Maharajah Vijay Sinhji of Rajpipla with two society ladies on the eve of World War II

number of them offered their subjects an administration far better than that which the British provided. A few were petty despots, more concerned with squandering their states' revenues in order to slake their own extravagant desires, than with improving the lot of their people.

With all the revenue, duties and taxes amassed in the states at their disposal, the princely rulers of India were uniquely placed to indulge their personal eccentricities. The 565 ruling princes could boast an average of 11 titles, 5.8 wives, 12.6 children, 9.2 elephants, 2.8 private railway cars, 3.4 Rolls Royces and 22.9 tigers killed.

In god-obsessed India, legend and folklore ascribed divine descent to some princes, with certain ruling dynasties tracing their ancestry on the flimsiest evidence and a great deal of imagination to the moon, the sun and even the Hindu gods. To gain credibility for these far-fetched fantasies and theories, mystical, elaborate spectacles, rituals and ceremonies were performed in front of their trusting subjects.

Many occupiers of these splendid palaces whiled away their time in the pursuit of two of their favourite pastimes, sex and sport. The harem was an integral part of the ruler's palace, whether Muslim or Hindu, and was regularly stocked with dancing girls and concubines. Rooms were devoted exclusively to housing the collection of tigers, panthers, elephants and various species of antelope killed by generations of princes in the jungles, not only of the state, but

from all over the world. Many of the reception rooms in the palaces were carpeted with the skins of tigers shot personally by the master of the palace. The harems have long gone, but the tiger skin trophies have remained, proudly displayed by succeeding generations. Many of the rulers were great sportsmen, acquiring international standards in cricket, polo, falconry and hunting. Falconry was a sport enjoyed by both sexes of the ruling families. Some became world authorities on obscure subjects like tiger shooting and cheetah coursing.

It was not all extravagance and eccentricity, however. Many of the rulers were highly educated and enlightened men, noted for their substantial achievements. Their subjects enjoyed benefits and privileges often different from those obtaining in areas administered directly by the British, and from state to state these might have included banning polygamy, equal status for women, making education free and universally available, efforts to elevate the status of the untouchables, the building of railways, dams, industries, parks, facilities for recreation and worship, and the embracing of advances in science. One particular state even enjoyed the benefit of no taxation! Sons of self-indulgent and flamboyant rulers turned the tables, ruling ably and responsibly to reform their states.

The independence movement led by Gandhi, Nehru, Patel and the Congress Party aimed for the unification of the country under a modern

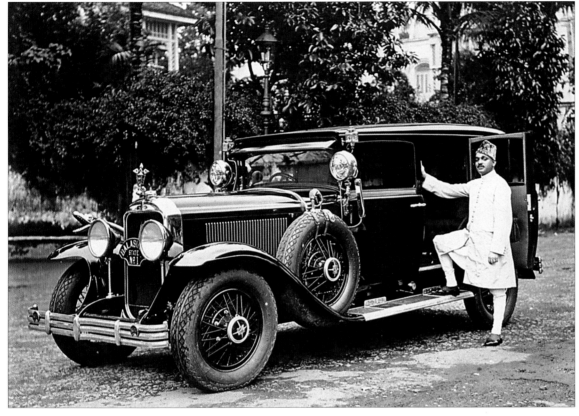

NAWAB SAHEB JAMAIYAT KHAN OF BALASINORE POSES PROUDLY WITH HIS BUICK

democratic political system. It sought to put an end to the princes' powers and to have their states merged into an independent India. Virtually overnight, and with clever political manoeuvring by Lord Mountbatten and Sardar Vallabhbhai Patel, the princes were stripped of their potency. One by one, the 565 ruling princes, the heirs of generations of rulers, signed the Act of Accession, relinquishing all their authority and joining the Indian Union. Not a single shot was fired and not one life lost, except that of the unfortunate prince who died of a heart attack immediately after signing. By the end of 1948AD the whole of the Indian subcontinent was unified, and autocracy gone forever.

In the 1970s AD the socialist leaning government further curtailed the limited powers which the princes still held. They were stripped of their titles, and their wealth was gradually to be eroded through taxation, abolition of privy purses and confiscation of property without compensation. The only legacies that remain are the forts and palaces, opulent and monumental reminders of the glorious princes' pasts.

The royal families, although stripped of their titles, were not however stripped of their dignity and ingenuity. Many have become successful politicians, academics and businessmen. Former hunters have become active and influential conservationists. Almost all have adapted admirably to life as ordinary citizens, and the royal families are looked upon with great respect and fondness by their former subjects. The head of the former ruling family is still addressed by many as "Bapa", reflecting the almost paternal relationship that had developed over the centuries between the rulers and the ruled.

Royal Families and Palaces of Gujarat confines itself to those princely states in Gujarat that have at least one palace open to tourists as an Heritage Hotel, museum or monument, and those that have registered as Heritage Hotel projects with the Heritage Hotels Association – Gujarat.

This book is an account of the Gujarati royal families and their palaces. Many are still their private residences. In many cases these palaces are in need of urgent repair and restoration. We should not forget that they are an important part of the heritage of both India and Britain, many palaces having been designed by once eminent British architects. It would be sad to lose this important part of our joint heritage.

Preface

Gujarat is India's westernmost state, bound to the west by a 1,660 kilometre long coastline, to the north by deserts, and to the east and south by mountain ranges including the Aravalis, Satpuras and the Western Ghats. Historically, the state comprised three cultural and geographic areas: Gujarat, which was the eastern belt of the existing state; Saurashtra, which comprised the massive Kathiawadi peninsula; and Kutch, the area between the northern coast of the Gulf of Kutch and Sindh, now a province of Pakistan. Saurashtra was one of India's most affluent regions, and its ports, fertile agricultural areas, rich pastoral grasslands and river valleys became one of prime targets for invaders, who came by the sea or through the north west frontier passes. Because of this incredible geographic diversity and affluence, the princely states of Gujarat were ruled by a number of different communities, unlike, for example, Rajasthan, where seventeen of the nineteen most important princely states were ruled by the Hindu Rajput community.

The Hindu Rajputs, who ruled the majority of the princely states in India from Kashmir in the Himalayas to Mysore in southern India, and regardless of whether the paramount power was Muslim, Hindu or British, were prominent in Gujarat as well, and the various Rajput clans – Jadejas, Jhalas, Gohils, Jethwas, Vaghela-Solanki and Chauhans – accounted for a considerable number of the princely states.

The Hindu Marathas were skilled mountain warriors, and took over the hills of southern Gujarat, making Baroda their seat of power.

The Hindu Kathis ruled parts of Kutch and Kathiawad for centuries, and continued their rule over states in the hinterland like Jasdan, Jetpur and Bhilka.

The Muslim Mughals, who were the overlords of almost all of India including Gujarat in the 16th and 17th centuries AD, appointed governors called subhedars, later Babis, who carved out independent states at Junagadh, Balasinore, Cambay and Radhanpur during the 18th century AD, as the Marathas set in train the downfall of Mughal supremacy in India. Of particular interest was the Afghan Lohani family, who ruled earlier from Jalore in southern Rajasthan, moving to Gujarat and setting up the state of Palanpur in the 16th and 17th centuries AD, and proving to be one of India's longest ruling Muslim dynasties.

The Portuguese naval forces were too powerful for the Muslim, Hindu and perhaps even British rulers, and the port of Daman and the island of Diu, captured in 1531AD and 1536AD respectively, remained with them long after the British lowered the Union Jack and retreated to London in 1947AD.

The Patels, who had become predominantly agricultural by occupation and were landowners rather than rulers, became rulers of the state of Patdi and of some smaller jagirs.

By the time of the Walker Settlement of 1807AD, the British were the established overlords of all of Gujarat, except for the Portuguese ports, and this included areas like Ahmedabad, Kheda and Surat. Other Europeans, notably the Dutch, did not rule Gujarat, but had been trading with Gujarat since about 1600AD, with factories in Surat, Baroda and the Sarkhej suburb of Ahmedabad.

The architecture of the palaces is equally diverse and interesting. The earlier palaces, called darbargadhs, were easily accessible to the subjects,

Preface

DARBARHALL IN BALASINORE OLD PALACE. THE PALACE WAS DAMAGED BY FIRE IN THE 1940S AD. THIS PHOTOGRAPH WAS SALVAGED FROM THE FIRE

A BANQUET AT BARODA, HELD IN HONOUR OF A BRITISH AGENT

and had high walls, often fortified by crenellations and bastions. The artisans of Gujarat were experts in wood and stone carving and embellished the palaces liberally with ornamental carved balconies called jarokhas, intricate fretwork windows called jalis, sculptures, reliefs, friezes, cusped arches and pillars. The architectural style was called Indo-Saracenic, a blend of Islamic geometry and Hindu ornamentation, and a style common to both Hindu and Muslim palaces in the 15th to 18th centuries AD.

The ruler had a paternal role and did not begrudge giving credit for the performance of the state to its citizens. Many a king, Hindu or Muslim, would have been destroyed without the support of Brahmin administrators and bania money lenders. Maharao Lakhpat Sinh called upon banias like Punja Seth, Rupsi Shah and Gordhan Mehta to save his treasury from breaking. The Jam sahebs depended on a bania to help them pay the cost of a prince's coronation when their treasury collapsed in the 17th century AD. The ruler of Porbandar gave a letter of recognition to a merchant who helped persuade Mughal emperors to reduce the levies on Porbandar. Baha-ud-din, a minister in the court of the nawabs of Junagadh, was honoured with a mausoleum more magnificent than those which the nawabs had reserved for themselves! Artists and artisans were given patronage and recognition.

The coming of the British brought a change in the attitude of the rulers. For their part, the British realised that the best way to control India was to win over the ruling dynasties, and to create a division between the rulers and the subjects. With the Europeanisation of the rulers, the concept of palaces changed. The darbargadhs were no longer residences, but just used as offices and courts, and the rulers moved to modern palaces called rajmahals or huzoor palaces, situated in the countryside, drawing heavily from European architecture. The

Gujarat

preferred style here was Venetian-Gothic, which had begun to see a revival in the late 19th century AD in England as well, for the thick walls, ornamental arches and domes were more in keeping with local tastes and weather conditions than the colonial period architecture of England, designed for the cold and rain. Even extensions to existing darbargadhs were done in the European style, and their haphazard symmetry is a delight to behold.

In Gondal, the lower floors of the Naulakha darbargadh are in the Indo-Saracenic style with lots of cusped arches, jarokha balconies and Hindu devotional sculptures. The top floor, added in the late-19th and early-20th centuries AD by HH Maharajah Bhagwat Sinhji, has pointed Gothic arches, trussed roofs and European busts. Yet the overall facade does not look in any way contradictory!

The interior reflects the exotica fashion of the times: rich embroideries and other textiles of Kutch and Kathiawad, brass chests, brass utensils and woodcrafts of Saurashtra, Indian paintings and excellent silverwork from Kutch and Rajkot. The princely rulers also imported the best marble from Italy, mirrors and stained glass from Belgium, heat resistant glass from Austria, teakwood from Burma, walnut furniture from Kashmir, chandeliers in blown glass and cut crystal from Venice, Belgium and Czechoslovakia, carpets and rugs from northern India and Persia, porcelain from China and Japan, crystal from Europe, and works of art from Rajasthan, Europe and south east Asia.

The states of Gujarat, both minor and major, were constantly at war with each other. The Walker Settlement of 1807AD, signed in Gujarat, brought peace and the rulers found time for sport. Blood sports, of course, were dominant – each prince would compete with a view to increasing the size of his trophy collection. Jam Saheb Digvijay Sinhji of Nawanagar would think nothing of shooting 1,000 brace of partridge in a season. HH Maharajah Krishna Kumar Sinhji of Bhavnagar kept 32 cheetahs for antelope coursing and patronised falconry. The Maharajah of Idar was known for his pigsticking safaris. HH Maharajah Amar Sinhji of Wankaner hosted duck shoots, and his grandsons, Yuvraj Dr Digvijay Sinh and Yuvraj Ranjit Sinh, used to collect trophies the world over.

Jam Saheb Ranjit Sinhji of Nawanagar and his nephew, Duleep Sinhji, excelled in cricket and

WEDDING PROCESSION OF THE PRESENT-DAY ROYALS OF RAJPIPLA

played for England, and HH Maharana Natwarsinhji of Porbandar captained India's first test team to England. Maharao Madan Sinhji of Kutch (who represented India) and Shiv Badhra Sinh of Bhavnagar were excellent tennis players. HH Maharajah Vijay Sinhji of Rajpipla was a talented horseman and polo player. His horses won prizes at the Irish Derby, the Epsom Derby and at the Belgian Grand Prix, and dominated the Indian racing season in the early-1930s AD.

Even today, some of these sporting traditions continue. Nawab Muhammad Salabat Khan Babi of Balasinore has a cabinet full of trophies won in heavy weight boxing, cricket, football, hockey and athletics. HH Maharajah Jyotendar Sinhji of Gondal and HH Maharajah Chaitanya Dev Sinhji of Wadhwan, are known names in motor sport, both with their ancestral cars at vintage and classic car rallies, and more recently with contemporary sports models. The Gaekwads of Baroda are a keen golfing family, and own golf clubs in Baroda and Bombay. The Maharajah of Idar has a good-sized stud farm of racing horses at his Himmatnagar palace. Darbar Saheb Satyajit Kumar Khaccher of Jasdan has a good stable of race-horses.

From the turn of the 20th century AD, an European education was considered essential for the elite – either by going to university in Europe, or by having private European tutors or by boarding in one of the public schools at Rajkot, Ajmer,

MAHARAJAH RAGHUVIR SINHJI OF RAJPIPLA ON HIS WEDDING DAY IN 1964AD

Dehradhun or Bangalore, which trained the students to be as English as the English. HH Maharajah Pratap Sinh of Wankaner went to Cambridge, and HH Maharana Mayurdhwaj Sinhji Megarajji the third of Dhrangadhra studied philosophy at Oxford. HH Maharajah Bhagwat Sinhji of Gondal was awarded Doctorates from Edinburgh and Oxford universities. The princesses of Palanpur studied under private tutors in the south of France, and Thakore Saheb Manohar Sinhji of Rajkot studied business

management in the United Kingdom.

Even foreign wives were in vogue, and some of these like the Australian wife of HH Nawab Saheb Sir Taley Muhammad Khan and the European wife of HH Maharana Natwarsinhji were officially recognised as their wives, albeit with new names, Begum Jahanara of Palanpur and Maharani Anant Kunverba of Porbandar!

But it was not all wine, women, song and decimated wildlife. Many of the rulers were also great administrators. The working day of the Maharao of Kutch and Maharana of Dhrangadhra began invariably at dawn, seldom ending before dusk. HH Maharajah Sayajirao Gaekwad of Baroda introduced railways, town planning and important education reforms – even today the Maharajah Sayajirao University (MSU) is well recognised in India. HH Maharajah Bhagwat Sinhji introduced free compulsory education, abolished taxes, commissioned irrigation networks, started railway connections and revamped town planning. Gondal today has wider roads in the town centre than other towns of its size. HH Maharajah Vijay Sinhji improved the quality of agricultural produce in Rajpipla, and during his rule the revenue of Rajpipla doubled in fifteen years. HH Maharajah Amar Sinhji introduced reforms and agricultural co-operatives.

Nationalism, too, showed itself in places. Even during the British period, rulers patronised Indian arts, music, poetry and literature. Visitors to the palaces of Gujarat need to understand that the value judgments of Indians are not the same as those of Europeans. Seeing a magnificent palace in an orchard near a cluster of small houses may seem incongruous, but Indians by nature are gregarious and prefer to live in crowded areas. A house in the centre of a downtown area may fetch the same, or even a better price than a beautiful terraced garden bungalow a few kilometres outside the town limits! Living on top of the shop may not be an

NAWAB SAHEB JUMAIYAT KHAN BABI OF BALASINORE WITH HIS DAUGHTERS

Englishman's idea of the ideal residence, but many middle-class Indian families prefer to convert the ground floor of their house into an office or shop, so that they can retire from the hot afternoon sun, when few buyers are about.

There has rarely been any resentment towards rulers, and no social revolution of the French kind. People accepted the ruler's spending as his income, in return for providing protection in the old days and administration in later days, and recognised that the spending on pleasures and palaces was just a minute fraction of the income of the state. Even now, the royal families are looked up to by locals.

The condition of the palaces, castles and mansions of Gujarat should not be measured by European standards. Natural calamities and climactic changes are extreme in Gujarat, as opposed, for

example, to England, and an excellent restoration job of a palace in the normally dry desert district of Kutch could be rendered null and void by heavy monsoon showers, a beautifully landscaped garden destroyed by a spell of drought, an expensive carpet spoiled by dust storms or an entire facade ravaged by a cyclone!

Importing matching replacements for stained glass or chandeliers from Europe, or getting them repaired locally, can be a difficult and expensive exercise for owners of palaces in India. Hence the blown glass Venetian chandeliers of Wankaner palace, broken during a storm many years ago, have never been repaired, and the gas lamps of the early-1900s AD New Engine car in Gondal have only recently been restored. Due to weather conditions, electrical failures and other problems are not uncommon, and many owners prefer to replace carefully concealed internal wiring or plumbing with exposed wires and pipes, which are easier to repair. Instead, visitors should focus their appreciation on the intricate architectural features, collections and ingenuity of these palaces, forts and mansions.

Gujarat had hundreds of rulers, ranging from the chieftain Veja-no-ness, who ruled over half a square mile and fewer than 200 subjects, to the Maharajah of Baroda, who reportedly ruled over some three million subjects, and the Maharao of Kutch, who held sway over more than one million square miles!

Gun Salute States of Gujarat and Saurashtra

21 GUN SALUTE STATE
BARODA   HH Maharajah
      Gaekwad:Hindu:Maratha

17 GUN SALUTE STATE
KUTCH   HH Maharao
      Jadeja:Hindu:Rajput

15 GUN SALUTE STATE
IDAR   HH Maharajah
      Rathore:Hindu:Rajput

13 GUN SALUTE STATES
BHAVNAGAR   HH Maharajah
      Gohil:Hindu:Rajput

DHRANGADHRA   HH Maharana
      Jhala:Hindu:Rajput

JAMNAGAR   HH Maharajah Jam
      Jadeja:Hindu:Rajput

JUNAGADH   HH Nawab Saheb
      Babi:Muslim:Afghan origin

PALANPUR   HH Nawab Saheb
      Lohani:Muslim:Afghan origin

PORBANDAR   HH Maharana
      Jethwa:Hindu:Rajput

RAJPIPLA   HH Maharajah
      Gohil:Hindu:Rajput

11 GUN SALUTE STATE
GONDAL   HH Maharajah (earlier Thakore Saheb)
      Jadeja:Hindu:Rajput

JAFRABAD   HH Nawab Sidi of Janjira
      Sidi:Muslim

KHAMBHAT   HH Nawab
      Shiya:Muslim

MORVI   HH Maharajah (earlier Thakore Saheb)
      Jadeja:Hindu:Rajput

WANKANER   HH Maharajah
      (earlier Thakore Saheb)
      Jhala:Hindu:Rajput

9 GUN SALUTE STATES
ALIRAJPUR   HH Raj
      Hindu:Rajput

BALASINORE   Nawab (earlier Nawab Saheb)
      Babi:Muslim:Afghan origin

BARIA   HH Raja
      Chauhan:Hindu:Rajput

CHOTTA UDAIPUR   HH Maharajah (also Raj)
      Chauhan:Hindu:Rajput

DHARAMPUR   HH Maharajah
      Parmar:Hindu:Rajput

DHROL   HH Thakore Saheb (also Maharaj Saheb)
      Jadeja:Hindu:Rajput

LIMBDI   Thakore Saheb
      Jhala:Hindu:Rajput

LUNAVADA   HH Raj
      Solanki:Hindu:Rajput

PALITANA   HH Maharajah (also Thakore Saheb)
      Gohil:Hindu:Rajput

RADHANPUR   HH Nawab
      Babi:Muslim:Afghan origin

RAJKOT   HH Thakore Saheb
      Jadeja:Hindu:Rajput

SACHIN   HH Nawab
      Muslim

SANTRAMPUR   HH Raj
      Hindu:Rajput

VANSDA   HH Raj (also Maharajah)
      Parmar:Hindu:Rajput

WADHWAN   HH Maharajah
      (earlier HH Thakore Saheb)
      Jhala:Hindu:Rajput

NON-SALUTE STATES
There were numerous non-salute states, including:
JASDAN   Darbar Saheb
      Khaccher:Hindu:Kathi

PATDI   Darbar Saheb
      Desai:Hindu:Patel

The above lists are in alphabetical order, and do not follow any order of precedence.

NOTE While we have tried to be accurate with titles, every ruler had a number of titles which could be up-graded. Titles given by the British could be different from those by which a ruler was addressed by his subjects. Similarly, the gun salutes could vary between a British organised function and a local function.

The Princely State of Balasinore

9 GUN SALUTE STATE

The Babi dynasty came to India from Afghanistan, and is said to have had humble beginnings as guards during the Mughal period. The fortunes of the Babis changed, goes a tale, when one of the guards saved the life of Mughal emperor Akhbar during a big cat hunt. According to another story, the Babis were given important positions following on the giving of military assistance to the Mughals. They were appointed governors of various regions of Gujarat, a coveted position at that time, for the fertile lands and ports of Gujarat brought in fabled levels of prosperity.

One of the governors, Subah Azam Khan, was responsible for building the Mughal palace in the Badhra fort of Ahmedabad during the 1630s AD, an imposing building with high arches and pretty balconies. So prolific was he as a builder that he was called Udai, the Indian name for termite, an invertebrate known for its intricate mounds.

By the mid-18th century AD, the Marathas had begun to prove themselves as major powers in India on the ruins of the Mughal empire, but there was no single national force between the fall of the Mughals and the British crown. The Babis took full advantage of this disarray and established their own princely states. The Subah of Ahmedabad, Salabat Khan Babi, took Balasinore between the green fields of Kheda

NAWAB SAHEB SHER KHAN BABI OF PALANPUR, GRANDFATHER OF THE PRESENT-DAY BEGUM OF BALASINORE, WITH HIS TWO SONS

and the hills of the Panchmahals, as Ahmedabad by then was a Maratha stronghold; the Subah or Fozdar of Sorath (Saurashtra), Muhammad Sher Khan (also called Bahadur Shah) made his capital at Junagadh; and other Babi rulers took Balasinore between the fertile river plains of Kheda and the Gulf of Cambay, and Radhanpur in northern Gujarat. Ironically, the youngest member of the family got Junagadh, the largest territory, and the eldest got Balasinore, the smallest territory!

By the time Nawab Saheb Sher Khan Babi in the 19th century AD came to the throne, the nawabs of Balasinore ruled around 180 square miles and commanded nine gun salutes. Further progress came to Balasinore under Nawab Saheb Jumaiyat Khan Babi, who introduced schools and hospitals. He was a great dramatist and poet, and unlike other Indian rulers, who under British influence had started keeping a distance from their subjects, would appear in public drama performances! "Those who have criticized the Indian rulers for staying away from their subjects in the 19th and 20th centuries AD would be surprised to know that my father's public appearances were not appreciated by the people of Balasinore!", Nawab Muhammad Salabat Khan Babi explained to me. "They actually complained to the British political agent that he was not keeping the

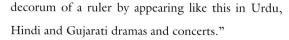

GARDEN PALACE

DRAWING ROOM AT THE GARDEN PALACE

decorum of a ruler by appearing like this in Urdu, Hindi and Gujarati dramas and concerts."

The present owner of the palaces, Nawab Muhammad Salabat Khan Babi came to the throne as a minor, and the Act of Accession was signed by HH Maharajah of Lunawada, who had been nominated to represent a number of young rulers in this area. His mother was appointed as his guardian. Nawab Muhammad Salabat Khan Babi went to school at Bishop's Cotton, Pune, and was a great athlete with many awards in sport like heavyweight boxing to his credit. His wife, Begum Farhat Sultana, says of her own education: "I went to school at Walsingham Convent, Bombay, and later joined my cousin, the Princess of Palanpur, in the south of France where we were privately educated. I have many hobbies – interior decorating, reading, flower arranging, cooking, painting . . ."

Their son and heir, Nawab Zada Sala-ud-din, goes to boarding school at Rajkumar College, and has won three gold medals for public speaking and recitation at national school level competitions, including one for repeating the speech of Sardar Vallabhbhai Patel, the man responsible for dismantling the princely order, something the family finds amusing! Nawab Muhammad Salabat Khan Babi has three daughters; Nawabzadi Meher Afshababi, the eldest, lives in San Francisco; the second, Nawabzadi Anjum Sultana, lives in Los Angeles; and the youngest, Nawabzadi Ahilya Sultana, is a keen collector of autographed photographs of former and existing royal families. "We were glad, in a way, that the privy purses were abolished," the nawab told me, "because had we depended on the Rs.60-65,000 we received from the government, it would not have been possible to maintain our lifestyle now. As the purses were stopped, we stopped expecting them, and worked at how to get a suitable income."

The darbargadh of Balasinore was a grand palace, with an elaborate darbarhall, illuminated by huge Venetian chandeliers that hung from decorated

Balasinore

MAQBARA OF NAWABS

MOSQUE BY THE OLD PALACE

NAWAB SAHEB JUMAIYAT KHAN BABI IN HIS WEDDING ATTIRE

ceilings, and carved wooden galleries from where events could be witnessed in the darbarhall. The palace was burnt down in the 1940s AD, following court intrigue involving their diwan, and the family now lives in the Garden palace, originally the minister's bungalow, set in acres of fruit orchards and agricultural fields.

The bungalow has a marble biradari and a fountain in the forecourt. The drawing room is beautifully furnished with Louis XIV style French chairs, antique furniture, portraits and photographs salvaged from the ruined palace, colourful carpets and a stuffed panther shot by Nawab Muhammad Salabat Khan Babi. The banqueting hall has a

Balasinore

GUEST ROOM AT THE GARDEN PALACE

THE OLD PALACE OF BALASINORE, BURNT IN THE 1940S AD

communal dining table set with matching chairs, cabinets housing trophies won by the nawab at various sporting events and autographed photographs collected by the nawab's daughter. A sofa set has a side table, on which are placed photograph albums of Balasinore. The four rooms downstairs are now open for tourists to stay as guests of the family, appointed in a mixture of old and new furniture. "We have our own vegetable garden, fruit orchards, poultry and cattle, and guarantee home grown food," explains the begum, "and visitors have appreciated the food, drawn from old nawabi recipes, and the way it is presented." Upstairs are the

family apartments, with beautiful cusped arches leading to a balcony with fine views. The European guesthouse, with trussed roofs, shares the same complex.

Across the road from the Garden palace gate is the Daria mahal palace, a lakeshore bungalow of about twenty-five rooms, with magnificent views over the water beside which the Mughal armies are said to have camped in the 17th century AD. The maqbara of the nawabs of Balasinore can also be seen on the lakeshore.

NAWAB SAHEB JUMAIYAT KHAN BABI OF BALASINORE

The Princely State of Baroda

**21 GUN
SALUTE STATE**

The princely state of Baroda emerged out of the 18th century AD surge of the Marathas, when they rose as the major national power in India on the ruins of the Mughal empire.

The Gaekwads were earlier military leaders under the powerful Maratha kings, called Peshwas, and were responsible for the conquest of Gujarat. The dynasty owes its origin to Damaji Gaekwad, a commander of the Maratha forces, who was responsible for many victories in fertile Gujarat and the Kathiawadi peninsula between 1717-20AD. His successor, Pillaji Gaekwad, made his headquarters at Songadh in south Gujarat and became in the 1720s AD a powerful military leader taking areas around the Mahi river, defeating Momin Khan of Surat and, in return for military assistance to the governor of Ahmedabad, was granted the chauth of south Gujarat. Pillaji was on the way to carving out an independent kingdom by taking Baroda with the help of the Desai jagirdars of Padra, but his attempt was foiled by a Rajput governor in Gujarat, Abhay Sinhji, by whom he was stabbed to death.

The work left undone by his father was completed by his son, Damaji the second, who captured Baroda in 1736AD and invaded Ahmedabad to avenge his father's death. The Muslims signed a treaty whereby the Gaekwads would receive a substantial share in the provinces of Gujarat. His expedition to collect the chauth from Saurashtra was successful, Borsad was conquered, and Baruch was invaded forcing the ruler to forge a treaty. By the 1760s AD, Damaji had taken vast areas of north Gujarat, including Patan, Visnagar, Kheralu and Vadnagar, and had conquered the Kathi stronghold of Amreli. The Gaekwads lost several skirmishes with the Peshwa overlords, resulting in their imprisonment or dethroning, but they always managed to regroup.

Fortunes improved for the Gaekwads in

THE LAXMI VILAS PALACE DOMINATES THE CITYSCAPE

1779AD when the East India Company went to war with the Peshwas. The Peshwa region of Gujarat was made out to the Gaekwad leader, Fateh Sinhji, and they were given the free rule of Baroda province on condition that they shared revenue and powers with the British and gave aid of 3,000 cavalry when needed.

Things were not all rosy, however. The Gaekwads had to face problems with the Peshwas, and there was internal conflict and intrigue. Ganpatarao, who came to the throne in 1847AD, initiated the progress of Baroda. He ruled peacefully and kept good relations with the British imperial power. The sale of children and female infanticide, prevalent in some communities, were banned, a central court was established, vaccines were introduced, and a railway line was commissioned in 1856AD.

His younger brother, Khanderao, succeeded him and helped the British crush a local mutiny. He tried to reform the army, abolished the exploitative jagirdari system of agriculture, and tried to separate the judiciary from its executive functions.

Sport was his passion – he loved hunting, wrestling and gymnastics. Architecture was another love, and palaces were commissioned during his rule.

More than anyone else, it was HH Maharajah Sayajirao Gaekwad, adopted heir of Khanderao, to whom Baroda even today owes its progress. He came to the throne as a minor in 1875AD and was given full powers in 1881AD. Immediately, he began the process of reform. The Gaekwads had a reputation for vanity and extravagance – they boasted diamonds larger than the Kohinoor, carpets set with pearls and cannon cast in gold and silver, but Sayajirao forced a progressive march away from feudalism. Roads and railways networked the state, and departments for agriculture, industry and commerce were set up to encourage cotton and other cash crops in rich Baroda soil, to develop a cotton industry, to commission banks and to encourage handicraft. Survey and settlement were organized, income tax was levied, a Stamp Act came into effect, the civil code was revised, and new penal, criminal and police codes were framed.

The maharajah believed that enlightenment was the path to progress. The new riches of the Baroda state were channelled to make education free and compulsory, to encourage libraries in cities, towns and villages and even to set up mobile libraries to carry books into the interior. Laws prohibiting bigamy and child marriages came into effect, and a legislative assembly was commissioned. A public works department was organized, and local self-government was revived. There was considerable progress in trade and industry, and the port of Okha, near Jamnagar, that had been taken from the Waghers by the Gaekwads in 1807AD, was developed. There was public awakening in the entire state of Baroda during his rule. Even his wife, the

RAJMAHAL (PALACE ROAD)

UPPER STOREY INTERIOR OF KIRTI MANDIR

Baroda

KIRTI MANDIR ROYAL MONUMENT

PRATAP VILAS PALACE AT LALBAGH, NOW THE RAILWAY STAFF COLLEGE

maharani, was active in championing the cause of Indian women, chairing a number of conferences on emancipation.

HH Maharajah Sayajirao Gaekwad became the third ruler of India, after the Nizam of Hydrabad and the Maharajah of Mysore, to be given a salute of twenty-one guns by the British government. He was flamboyant too, and spent lavishly on palaces, art collections, hunting trips, and race horses. Fights were staged between buffalo, elephant and other animals. Reverend Edward Weedon, in *A Year with the Gaekwar of Baroda*, said that the maharajah lived in the magnificent style expected of a ruler in the

orient, but his expenses were a trifle compared to that spent on public services. He was, Weedon felt, like a democratic monarch who had a council, a judiciary and a legislature to guide him. It did not take long, he explained, to judge the maharajah's wise use of the state's riches. Caine, in *Picturesque India* gave the following figures: land revenue £8.5 million, customs £94,000, trade taxes £31,000, liquor and opium tax £42,000, forests £7,000, tributes from other states £64,000, and justice £26,000.

Sayajirao's grandson, HH Maharajah Pratap Sinhji, was in every way as much a wastrel as his

grandfather was a great ruler. Except in matters of the turf, he had no great knowledge or insight. He broke the law set by his grandfather and married twice. Subjects were unhappy during his rule.

In 1948AD, the maharajah was among the first set of rulers to join the Indian Union, thanks to good advice from his diwans, but there was considerable hesitation before finally joining Bombay state in 1949AD. The maharajah fell from grace because of his apparent lack of patriotism. The privy purse was a hefty Rs.2.5 million!

HH Maharajah Pratap Sinhji's son, Fateh Sinhji, was a man of varied interests including sport, wildlife

Baroda

WINDOW SURROUND PAINTING BY NANDLAL BOSE, A FAMOUS BENGALI ARTIST

family also has vast industrial and other business interests, including one of the largest rayon producing units in Gujarat.

The oldest extant palace in Baroda is the three storey Nazzar Bagh palace, built in 1823AD, but it is in a somewhat derelict and dilapidated condition. Despite being owned by the royal family, it does not reflect any of the glory of the times when collared cheetahs stood on the steps, carpets were set with jewels and the family housed its fabulous diamonds there. Another palace, the Khanderao palace, is now the municipal office.

The Baroda family lives in the Laxmi vilas palace, commissioned by HH Maharajah Sayajirao Gaekwad

in the 1880s AD. The palace was designed by Major Mant, whose rather eclectic styles had given him the title of 'Mad Mant', and was completed by Chisolm after Mant's death. The palace took twelve years to build and cost £18 million.

The intention of the two architects was clear – they realised that the royals of Baroda needed a palace that could be used for state functions and western style living, but which at the same time should not ignore the traditions of having separate public areas, a zanana for the women and the maharajah's private apartments. The architecture is extraordinary – Indian and European architecture meet in one of the finest extravaganzas of domes,

conservation and the arts. He made many friends on his trips abroad and was well respected by the people. He was president of the World Wildlife Fund – India, and manager of the Indian test cricket team, and his wife was involved with the Gujarat kennel club in Baroda. After his death in the 1970s AD, Ranjit Sinhji, his brother, inherited the palaces. Ranjit Sinhji is a keen politician and has represented Baroda in various assemblies. Classical music and folk dances are two of his passions, and concerts and performances are often organized in the palace. His son, Samarjit, is now setting up a golf club and sports complex in the palace precincts. The Baroda

SHIV MAHAL PALACE

BUST OF HH MAHARAJAH SHIVAJIRAO GAEKWAD, FOUNDER OF THE SHIV MAHAL PALACE

cupolas, turrets, porticos, arches and decoration. The style drew from Mughal palaces, Rajput palaces like the Bharatpur fort palace, Jain temples, Venetian-Gothic facades and even classical art.

The main building materials are red sandstone from Agra, inlaid with the blue trapstone of Maharashtra and marble from Rajasthan. The interiors are equally delightful in their profusion of Carara marble, Venetian mosaic, stained glass, porcelain and other decoration. A huge portico leads to an impressive staircase, and upstairs are the maharajah's apartments. Three courtyards divide the palace, the floors are laid in mosaic with European

statues, and fountains and palm trees abound, the whole overlooked by galleries. The family has an extensive library and a billiard room. Royal portraits, most of them featuring HH Maharajah Sayajirao Gaekwad, line the walls. The darbarhall is one of the grandest in scale, with exquisite carved cedar galleries from where women looked down on events in the hall of audiences, with its distinctive multi-domed ceiling, Venetian mosaic floors, brass busts of the Maharajah of Baroda, the coat of arms and a silver throne. Behind the hall is a Venetian mosaic painting portraying a Maharashtrian wedding being blessed by European angels. The palace is set in 720 acres of land, filled with shade giving trees, and was landscaped by a Mr Gonderling from Kew Gardens.

The Motibagh school in the palace complex has now been turned into a museum and art gallery run by the family. As HH Maharajah Sayajirao Gaekwad knew little about art, he appointed a team to enhance his collection. The collection includes oil paintings by Ravi Varma, a prince of Travancore who took up painting; Venetian sculpture by Augusto Felici, sculpture by P Bose and portraits by Fyzee Rahman; an inlaid door, together with chandeliers and furniture salvaged from the three storey Renaissance style Makarpura palace when it was taken over by the Indian Air Force; not to mention portraits of the royal family, works by Lucas, Giovvani Costa, Wimperis, Charles Giron, GD Deuskar, Angelica Kauffman and minor artists, copies of great European

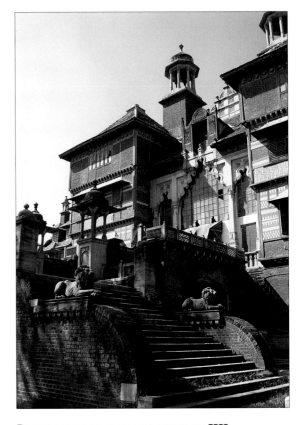

BARODA MUSEUM PURPOSE BUILT BY HH MAHARAJAH SAYAJIRAO GAEKWAD OF BARODA

artists, and oriental art from China and Japan.

The Pratap vilas palace at Lalbagh is now the Railway Staff College, with beautifully maintained gardens. The palace has Baroque style domes, classical columns and Venetian-Gothic features, which are still well maintained. Shiv mahal palace, founded by HH Maharajah Shivajirao Gaekwad, a relative, is in the Indo-Saracenic style with huge dome and arches. Inside is an impressive marble staircase flanked by paintings. The old banqueting hall has a set of walnut furniture including a long dining table, matching carved chairs and an intricate screen.

The Princely State of Bhavnagar

**13 GUN
SALUTE STATE**

**GATE AND FORECOURT AS SEEN FROM THE
ENTRANCE OF THE BHAV VILAS PALACE**

Unlike the Gohils of Udaipur, who belong to the solar clan, the Gohil dynasty of Bhavnagar claimed descent from the moon god. The Gohils came to the southern coastline of the Kathiawadi peninsula (Saurashtra) from Khergadh by the river Luni in the Marwar desert region of Rajasthan, following disputes with the Rathore Rajput rulers of Marwar. The leader of the clan, Sejakaji, was given the jagir of Ranpur by Khengarji, the ruler of Junagadh, in the mid-13th century AD. His grandson, Mokhdaji, developed the kingdom, further driving away the Kolis from Umrala and the Muslims from Gogha, and made Piram island a base for operations.

The history, however, remained turbulent, and constant battles, sieges and internal skirmishes made the family change capitals very often. Mokhdaji himself was a victim of one of these battles – he died when the powerful forces of Sultan Muhammad Tuglaq from Delhi invaded Gogha in 1349AD, but the territory was once again taken by his son, Vibhoji, in 1370AD. Vibhoji's son, Kanoji, who succeeded him, died when his son, Sarangji, was a minor, and the throne was usurped by his uncle.

Sarangji appealed for help to the ruler of Pawagadh and won back his throne.

A few generations later, Visoji came to the throne and received Sihore as a gift from the Audichya Brahmins and made it his capital, from which he ruled from 1570-1600AD. But Sihore was lost by his son, Dhunoji, in a battle with the Kathis. Dhunoji's successors, Ratanari and Harbhamji, also lost their lives fighting the powerful Kathi forces between 1611-22AD. Harbhamji's brother, Govindji, seized the throne from his nephew and rightful heir, Akherajji, who fled to Kutch, and Govindji gifted Gogha to the Mughal emperors in return for military assistance. Akherajji had his revenge, though, when he joined forces with the Kathi darbars and made another attack on Satrasal, the son and successor of his uncle, Govindji, and took back the kingdom after kidnapping Satrasal in his sleep.

Bhavnagar was founded by Akherajji's grandson, Bhav Sinhji, who had withstood many sieges on the darbargadh of Sihor. The city was founded in 1723AD, and under Bhav Sinhji, after whom it is named, and being on the seashore, grew into an

ABOVE AND TOP RIGHT:
THE DARBARGADH OF THE ROYAL FAMILY OF BHAVNAGAR, NOW A BANK, WAS AN OLD FORT, EXTENDED ACCORDING TO A DESIGN BY SIR WILLIAM EMMERSON, A PROMINENT ARCHITECT IN THE 1890S AD

THE OLD LIVING ROOM OF THE ROYAL FAMILY OF BHAVNAGAR, NOW THE ENTRANCE LOBBY OF THE NILAMBAGH PALACE HOTEL

NILAMBAGH PALACE HOTEL, WITH CANNON IN THE FORECOURT

COURTYARD OF NILAMBAGH PALACE HOTEL

important port. Bhav Sinhji made important trade treaties with other rulers and rid the Gulf of Cambay of its fierce sea pirates. He reconquered Gogha port from the local representatives of the Mughal empire, and took control of Sultanpur, which was then infested with pirates, and Trapai from Palitana. He started the first associations with the British by signing trade treaties with the East India Company in 1760AD. His successors continued their war against piracy, helping the Marathas on the eastern coast of the Gulf of Kutch and the East India Company at Surat.

The kingdom was expanded by Vakhat Sinhji towards the end of the 18th century AD when he conquered Talaja, Mahuva, Rajula, Kundla, Gadhada and Botad from the Nawab of Cambay, the Khumans and the Khasios, and forced Dedan of Danta to offer up Nazrana. He defeated a combined army of Kathi darbars at Chital, and repelled attacks from Palitana in 1775AD. He even entered into a battle with the nawabs of Junagadh, but the rulers of Porbandar intervened and a peace treaty was formulated in 1776AD. In 1802AD, the treaty of Vasai brought Bhavnagar under the control of the East India Company. There were differences with the Kheda representatives of the company on certain issues, and thus some parts of that state were confiscated in 1816AD.

Peace finally reigned in Bhavnagar after a peaceful settlement was made with the Kathis who had threatened hostilities in 1828AD. Sadul Khasia of Monpur, who had plundered the villages of Bhavnagar and taken shelter in the Gir forests in 1836AD, was brought to book by the Junagadh nawabs because of pressure from the British political agents. Gaurishankar Oza, who became diwan of Junagadh, proved to be an able diplomat, and settled important disputes. HH Maharajah Jeswant Sinhji, who came to the throne in 1854AD, helped the British armies to embark at Gogha port and to proceed to Ahmedabad, and in return got important trade rights for Bhavnagar port.

By 1866AD Gaurishankar diwan had settled the jurisdiction of 116 villages and the path was paved for HH Maharajah Takhat Sinhji, best known as the

Bhavnagar

builder of Bhavnagar and successor to HH Maharajah Jeswant Sinhji, to make Bhavnagar one of the foremost states of Saurashtra.

The revenue systems were revamped, schools for boys and girls were introduced, Gaurishankar lake was excavated, Alfred High School was inaugurated, Barton library was commissioned, Port Victor was started at Pipavav, and railways to Wadhwan and Dhoraji were introduced. In 1885AD Bhavnagar became the proud owner of the first Arts college of Saurashtra. The judiciary system was introduced during HH Maharajah Takhat Sinhji's rule. Sir William Emmerson, an architect of considerable importance, and one-time president of the Royal Institute of British Architects, whose other works in India were the Victoria memorial in Calcutta and Crawford market in Bombay, was commissioned to design a number of buildings, including a magnificent hospital, now known as Takhat Sinhji hospital.

HH Maharajah Bhav Sinhji succeeded HH Maharajah Takhat Sinhji in 1896AD, and though he did not approve of the flamboyance and extravagance of his father, followed HH Maharajah Takhat Sinhji's example in making Bhavnagar a progressive state. He started important relief measures to combat drought and plague in some parts of Bhavnagar state, introduced a people's representative committee comprising farmers, traders, municipal representatives and relatives of the

THE NILAMBAGH PALACE HOTEL STILL RETAINS FOURTEEN ACRES OF GROUNDS, EVEN AFTER HAVING HAD MUCH OF ITS LAND SOLD

family, and started a co-operative movement in 1917AD. Here again, as in the case of his ancestors, he had a good diwan, Prabhashankar Pattani. Being a teetotaller, HH Maharajah Bhav Sinhji introduced the prohibition of liquor in Bhavnagar state.

HH Maharajah Krishna Kumar Sinhji came to the throne as a minor in 1917AD, and the diwan and British agents controlled the state until he came of age. His rule saw the introduction of a number of movements for the betterment of the people. Mahatma Gandhi, who went to university in Bhavnagar, set up a school, Rastriya shala, and the self-government system was introduced in some villages as an experiment. For the first time in India, the Kjaraj committee was commissioned to look into the heavy debts of the farmers at Bhavnagar. The burden of taxation was reduced and a legislative assembly, albeit with modest powers, called Dharasabha, was established to discuss taxes and other needs of the people. Jagirs like Lathi and Vala were merged into the state in 1943AD under the Attachment Scheme.

Bhavnagar

THE BANQUETING HALL OF THE NILAMBAGH PALACE HOTEL

residences. The main palace is entered through huge arches, flanked by a facade of pillars and projecting balconies. The building is now the State Bank of Saurashtra, and most of the facade that survives is the extension designed by Sir William Emmerson.

The family now resides in a bungalow by the Nilambagh palace, commissioned to a German architect in 1859AD by HH Maharajah Jeswant Sinhji. The palace was built as the residence of Bhav Sinhji, then the crown prince – it is said that he did not approve of his father's lust for wine and women, and was banished to the new palace! Subsequent extensions were made: the palace became a royal guesthouse and later the royal residence. Magnificent carved arch gates lead into the palace, which was set in a huge complex of woods, gardens, orchards, lawns, outhouses and wells, of which some

When Independence came, there was pressure from many Hindu and Muslim rulers to join Pakistan, which was giving more attractive privileges to the princes, but being a staunch Hindu and patriot (leaders of Bhavnagar were among the most vociferous during the freedom struggle), he was one of the first rulers to join the Indian Union. He was later made Up-Rajpramukh of the United States of Saurashtra, and appointed governor of Madras.

HH Maharajah Krishna Kumar Sinhji and his brothers were keen hunters, but began a progression towards conservation. A cheetah, rather than guns,

would be taken for hunting blackbuck antelope. The cheetah would stand in a bullock cart with two trainers and a driver; when unleashed, the cheetah would chase the antelope, which would either escape unhurt, or be killed. Similarly, falcons or gun dogs were preferred over rifles. When rifles were used, there would be limited shooting, rather than indiscriminate firing.

The oldest extant palace of Bhavnagar, the darbargadh, was probably begun by Bhav Sinhji in the 1720s AD, and is in the centre of the city – many of the outhouses are now shops and humble

THE 1950s AD LIBRARY OF THE NILAMBAGH PALACE HOTEL

Bhavnagar

40,000 square feet have been retained by the family, providing a good facade against the city bustle, the rest having been sold.

Stepped arches run the complete length of the palace, which is built from stone mined at nearby Rajula. The portico at the entrance has a row of carved European style arches, and is flanked by cannon. Steps lead up to a majestic door framed by arches of beautifully carved teak wood. The living room of the palace, which now acts as the hotel lobby, has an intricate ceiling looking down on plush settees, exotically patterned carpet, Chez and other chandeliers, stuffed panthers, antique tables and life-size portraits of former royals of Bhavnagar. In the centre of the palace is a pleasant open courtyard, with fountains which are not operational at present, enclosed by colonnades and galleries. A scale model of the palace stands in a corner. The walls along the courtyard are adorned with European prints and line art. The library beside the courtyard was made in the 1950s AD with exquisite furniture, encasing hard backed books and paintings by Indian and foreign artists. The banqueting hall now functions as the restaurant and is still furnished with carved Burmese teak tables, elegant teak chairs, old side tables, cabinets, oil paintings by European and American artists, some of whom stayed at the palace, Chez chandeliers, Belgian mirrors, African stuffed birds and ivory objects. Beside it is a hall rented out for conferences with a marble floor and hunting trophies. A map of Bhavnagar state and the family tree can be seen in the hall.

A sweeping marble staircase leads up to the first floor. It is lined with paintings of cheetah coursing, and of old buildings of Bhavnagar, and with attractive illustrations of birds. The first and second floors of the palace offer accommodation in huge, high ceilinged rooms, some of them with original furniture dating from the days when it was occupied by the royal family. The swimming pool outside the palace is in a curious mix of Art Deco and Roman styles with steps and colonnades – it could almost be mistaken for a Roman bath. The site also offers facilities for tennis and table-tennis.

The sports club of the royal family, though, was the Bhav vilas palace, some distance from the Nilambagh. The Bhav vilas palace is splendidly situated facing lake Gaurishankar, and is entered by a huge crested wrought iron gate cast at Dublin. There is a long, rectangular lily pond with fountains in the forecourt leading to the main building, which has a massive portico and steps starting from an arch. The three drawing rooms are lined with stuffed animals from different countries of the world shot by the present owner and resident, Shiv Badhra Sinhji, son of HH Maharajah Krishna Kumar Sinhji and younger brother of Vir Badhra Sinhji, whose widow, Rajmata Brijraj Nandini, and son, HH Maharajah Vijayraj Sinhji, now own the Nilambagh. The courtyard to the rear leads to a lawn facing the lake.

HH MAHARAJAH VIJAYRAJ SINHJI WITH RAJMATA BRIJRAJ NANDINI

The palace has tennis courts, squash courts, a billiard room, a boat house, a swimming pool and many other sports facilities.

Near the palace is Victoria park, a huge patch of scrubland that once provided the family with game. Now, most of the indigenous wildlife is gone, but some antelope and hyena remain, along with extensive birdlife. The park is overlooked by the Dilbahar palace, residence of the late Kumar Shree Dharam Kumar Sinhji – the younger brother of HH Maharajah Krishna Kumar Sinhji – who was known for his falconry pursuits, knowledge of natural history and books, and as author of articles and scientific papers on the birds and wildlife of Saurashtra. The palace now belongs to his widow and daughter, who married into the Gondal family.

The Bhavnagar royals believed in quantity rather than quality. While no individual palace could match those of Junagadh, Wankaner, Kutch or Baroda, they had a number of properties for different purposes – for residences or guesthouses, or for sports, recreation, or entertaining. Many of these impressive buildings are now either demolished or owned by the government or private individuals. Many recreational country mansions were built by the seashore, for example Hatabh bungalow, Gopnath bungalow and Chanch island palace, the last two of which are still owned by the family; and in the forests, including one which is now a Forest Department rest house.

Rajmata Brijraj Nandini has won awards for her work in promoting education, and she is one of the most successful Heritage Hotel owners in India. The family moved to Bombay, for the sake of HH Maharajah Vijayraj Sinhji's children's education, but, once they board, the family will move to Bhavnagar. "I went to boarding school in Simla, a hill station in the Himalayas, and my family too came from a Himalayan kingdom," Maharani Samyukta Devi explains, "and so I am happier in Bhavnagar than in a large metro like Bombay. I would like to settle here, perhaps to write, and paint. My children love it here in the holidays. We are trying to give Nilambagh the look of a palace rather than an hotel. Once we move here, we should be able to create the right atmosphere. Bhavnagar was always progressive where women were concerned. My in-laws were so nice, that in the days when a heavy dowry was the norm during royal weddings, they did not ask for anything."

INNER COURTYARD OF THE NILAMBAGH PALACE HOTEL

TROPHY ROOM OF THE BHAV VILAS PALACE

FRONT ENTRANCE HALL OF THE NILAMBAGH PALACE HOTEL

The Princely State of Chotta Udaipur

9 GUN SALUTE STATE

THE MEDIEVAL WALLS OF CHAMPANER, CAPITAL OF THE CHAUHAN RAJPUTS BEFORE THEY LOST TO THE MUSLIMS IN THE 16TH CENTURY AD AND RETREATED TO THE HILLS OF CHOTTA UDAIPUR

KUSUM VILAS PALACE, BUILT IN THE 1930s AD IN THE INDO-SARACENIC STYLE

Chotta Udaipur was a second class state, with 525 villages, an income of Rs.2.5 million, cavalry, infantry, bodyguards and cannon, situated in the hills between Gujarat and Malwa. The state was ruled by the Chauhan dynasty, also called the Kheechi family, which was reputed to be one of the bravest Rajput clans in India.

The Chauhans colonised eastern Rajasthan in the 8th century AD, and were a major national power in northern India, ruling a huge tract of land from Nagpur and Ajmer in Rajasthan to Delhi. To conquer the prosperous Indo-Gangetic plains, the outposts of the cross-desert merchant caravan routes in Rajasthan and the rich coastline of Gujarat, an invader would first have to deal with the Chauhans. Many are the tales of the battles between the Chauhans and Muslim invaders like Muhammad Ghazni and Muhammad Ghori, with the Chauhan kings standing in the way of the Turks taking the whole of India; until the 12th century AD when Pritviraj Chauhan, whose exploits are part of much Indian bardic poetry, lost in battle to Muhammad Ghor, a sultan he had beaten in earlier conflicts, but pardoned, at the battle of Tarian in 1192AD. With none of the considerations of Rajput chivalry, the sultan had him blinded and put to the sword, so ending Rajput rule in Delhi.

But in the areas where they ruled, the Chauhans wielded considerable power. Among these were the Kheechi Chauhan chieftains who ruled petty states along the river Narmada, mentioned in 8th to 13th centuries AD references. They conquered the historic fort of Champaner, situated on a rocky mountain peak and guarded by natural rocky defences. The fort is said to have been built by the Bhil chieftain, Champa, but named after the powerful Chauhan ruler, Palandeo, though, according to some, after Lord Hanuman, a Hindu god, also called Pawanputra, who in the Ramayana, one of the great epic poems of the Hindu religion, carried a hill of the Himalayas to Lanka and dropped en route a piece of rock which is Pawagadh; and, to others, the strong winds (pawan meaning wind in Hindi) that blow in the high hills.

Sultan Ahmed Shah, who founded Ahmedabad in 1414AD, devastated Chauhan territories but could not lay siege to the fort. He tried again, but his one year siege had to be raised. Gujarati ballads describe the fort as home of the Ramayana and Mahabharata heroes, with wells of oil, massive stocks of grass, wood, corn, cloth, gold, ornaments and weaponry; and impregnable. Sultan Muhammad Shah, a successor of Ahmed Shah, spent six years getting ready for a siege on Pawagadh. In 1449AD, a letter from the sultan reached King Gangadas, asking him to make truce and pay tribute like other Rajput chiefs. The king accepted the challenge and played dice until the hour of battle approached. The queen had left the temple, and performed ceremonies before the siege was called on Champaner. The Rajput armies were out in full glory – and no less than 5,000 members of the sultan's cavalry and top military officers were killed.

Again, an order was received from the sultan, and sent through messengers of Virama, Rajput ruler of Idar, and Bagalana, another Hindu kingdom in present-day Maharashtra, instructing the king that it was the order of the sultan not to give refuge to Rajput chiefs, and warning him that the sultan had conquered many forts. Gangadas had the message washed with holy water. He held these two kings in no high regard – for they had agreed to give their daughters in marriage to the sultan, and in true Rajput tradition, death was preferable to dishonour. He gave a mocking reply to the message. The sultan touched his beard and vowed to avenge this insult.

Gangadas, in full armour, attacked the sultan's armies as they began to climb the fort, cutting off

GALLERY ABOVE THE PORTICO AT KUSUM VILAS PALACE

the head dresses and hair of the leaders, but not killing them. Virama, who was one of the leaders of the sultan's army, used a map of the fort approach drawn from pen pictures of visitors to Pawagadh, and had formed a strategy to invade the fort: foot soldiers to scale the walls, horsemen to protect the camp, elephants to batter down the defences, and rocks to be thrown by climbers from above the fort – but the attempt was foiled, and the soldiers were thrown down. The Khilji sultans of Mandu were in favour of the Rajputs of Champaner, as a buffer between them and the sultans of Ahmedabad, and

had supported them in the defence of the fort. The generals of Gangadas were in favour of a counter offensive as the sultan's army fled, but Gangadas himself said it would be cowardly to attack a fleeing army.

In 1459AD, Muhammad Bhegada was crowned and became known as a master of sieges, as he took the magnificent Junagadh fort. In 1483-84AD, he laid siege to Champaner. Knowing that conquest of the fort by direct assault was impossible, he created a new town called Mahmudabad, next to Champaner, with a view of Pawagadh. Twenty months later, he

Chotta Udaipur

saw his chance, and, observing that the guards were not on watch, ordered his armies to overpower them and enter the fort. Patai Rawal, the king of Champaner, knew that defeat was inevitable and prepared his people for the Rajput act of jauhar – death rather than dishonour. The women immolated themselves, so they would not be touched by alien hands, and the men, attired in saffron, jumped down on the invading army, injuring and killing hundreds of soldiers. Patai Rawal was taken prisoner and given the choice of converting to Islam or death – the brave Hindu king chose the latter.

Patai Rawal's surviving sons took refuge at Hamph in the hills, and his grandson from a pre-deceased son, Pritviraj Sinh, started a new chiefdom at Mohan, from where his descendants ruled before moving to Chotta Udaipur. In 1813AD, Rawal Rai Sinhji fortified Chotta Udaipur and built a fort and a palace for himself. He made a settlement with the

TROPHIED WILD CAT, KUSUM VILAS PALACE

RELIGIOUS PAINTING IN THE DRAWING ROOM, KUSUM VILAS PALACE

Marathas, who had become a powerful force on the national front, and agreed to pay tribute to the Gaekwads of Baroda. His son, Pritviraj Sinh the second, made an agreement with the British government in 1822AD for additional protection from the Marathas.

The golden age for Chotta Udaipur came when HH Maharajah Fateh Sinhji succeeded him in 1895AD. To the little known four tribal talukas in the hills of Chotta Udaipur, HH Maharajah Fateh

Sinhji brought progress and prosperity. He personally attended office and handled state affairs. By 1923AD, when he died, Chotta Udaipur was endowed with a number of modern buildings, railway connections, halls of audiences, palaces, a gymkhana club house, secretariat, hospitals, schools, including one for girls, and waterworks. Surveys were made, and new villages were settled.

His successor, HH Maharajah Natwar Sinhji, was renowned for his commitment to charitable causes. His public charity was known for its daily donations. He died in 1946AD in Lisbon, and his son, HH Maharajah Virendra Sinhji, came to the throne as a minor. During the merger of the princely states and the formation of the Indian Union, the Act of Accession was signed by guardians, including HH Maharajah of Lunawada.

HH Maharajah Virendra Sinhji is involved in a number of businesses. He owns a garment factory in

KUWARANI AMRIT MANJULI SINHJI AND KUMAR SAHEB BHAVANI PRATAP SINHJI

HH Maharajah Natwar Sinhji of
Chotta Udaipur

HH Maharajah Jeet Sinhji of Chotta Udaipur

Chotta Udaipur

ONE OF THREE MARBLE STATUES WHICH FORM THE CENTREPIECE OF A FOUNTAIN IN THE GROUNDS OF THE KUSUM VILAS PALACE

ORIGINAL ELEVATION OF THE KUSUM VILAS PALACE IN THE 1930s AD

Bangalore, a theatre in Chotta Udaipur and marble and granite works in Ambaji, is a director in the Tata group and has investments in a number of other industries. "I have started work on converting Kusum vilas palace into an Heritage Hotel," explains HH Maharajah Virendra Sinhji, "and I hope it will be done by the end of 1999AD. Unlike other property owners who are either doing it themselves or have given their properties to chains, I am planning a combination. The property will be owned by us, and we will look after the guests personally, but we will have some professionals involved."

HH Maharajah Virendra Sinhji's second son, Kumar Saheb Bhavani Pratap Sinhji, says: "Like other princely states, Chotta Udaipur had its hill station bungalows, and we have one in Mussourie. I am interested in converting that into an Heritage Hotel." As his wife, Kuwarani Amrit Manjuli Sinhji, puts it: "Not everyone is blessed with a heritage like ours, and not to maintain your properties is a waste. A huge staff is required to maintain a palace, and it is really only economically feasible if you take it up as a commercial venture like a hotel. I am from a city in Nepal, and it is difficult to live in a village like Chotta Udaipur unless you have some occupation – like an Heritage Hotel. Right now we have a house in Baroda and only drop in here occasionally."

Chotta Udaipur has many palaces. The old fort is now the subject of litigation with the government, and other palaces have been given for schools and

Chotta Udaipur

DRAWING ROOM, KUSUM VILAS PALACE

PAWAGADH FORT ON THE HILL

THE HISTORIC PAWAGADH FORT OF THE CHAUHAN RAJPUT DYNASTY OF CHOTTA UDAIPUR

hostels. The present family residence is the Kusum vilas palace, built in the 1930s AD during the rule of HH Maharajah Natwar Sinhji, in a style that is predominantly Indo-Saracenic, rather than in the European architectural style that was so popular in the period. The palace is set in forty acres of grounds, and is entered through a majestic wrought iron crested gate. The lawn in front has as the centrepiece a fabulous fountain with three massive marble statues of European women rising up from the centre of the water. Beside the lawn is the Shalimar, a Mughal style fountained garden. The facade is dominated by a huge dome flanked by smaller domes and turrets. A massive portico with cusped arches marks the entrance, and marble steps lead to a reception area with intricate filigree work on stone, the whole housing a sofa set, a glass cabinet guarding historic books, and big cats duly stuffed. The drawing room is beautifully attired in French period furniture, Belgian crystal chandeliers, marble Italian statues, stuffed animals and exotically coloured carpets. Paintings here depict religious Indian themes and old scenes of Chotta Udaipur. The games room displays an elderly billiard table.

The banqueting hall has a long communal table with matching chairs. A marble staircase leads upstairs, where another drawing room is resplendent with beautiful furniture and paintings. Art Deco furnished bedrooms and a bar room run the length of the first floor. A colourfully floored verandah offers views of the hills. The old guesthouse, the Prem Bhuvan, beside the palace, has a collection of royal portraits and pictures. The indoor swimming pool, housed in a special structure to give privacy to the royal family, is enclosed by carved pillars.

The Princely State of Dhrangadhra

13 GUN SALUTE STATE

The Jhala Rajput family of Dhrangadhra traces its history to the Makwana clan of warriors in Baluchistan, which ruled a number of villages near Nagar Parkar in Sindh. Hardevpal Makwana, of Kirantigarh in Sindh, travelled down to Anhilpataka (now Patan), which was the capital of the Solanki Rajput empire, spanning the whole of what is now Gujarat and parts of Rajasthan and Madya Pradesh, in the 12th century AD. He received as a gift from Raja Karan Solanki, probably in return for military assistance, 2,400 villages in the Kathiawadi peninsula. He set up capital at Patdi, at the north eastern edge of the peninsula, near the Little Rann of Kutch, with the blessings of the Shakti manifestations of the Hindu mother goddesses. The foremost temple of the patron goddess, Kul devis, of the Jhala dynasty, still occupies the northern point of the Patdi fort, though the capital of the Jhalas changed from Patdi to Kuva when Jet Sinhji became ruler of Zalawad (a Jhala kingdom in the 13th century AD).

By the end of that century, the Delhi sultan, Alla-ud-din Khilji, established his rule in Gujarat, defeating the Solanki kings, and appointing a subhedar to rule from Patan. The subhedar declared himself the independent sultan of Gujarat, and during the 15th century AD the new sultanate was founded, forcing many of the Hindu and Muslim kings to accept its rule. Sultan Ahmed Shah of this dynasty moved his capital from Patan to a new and more impressive city of Ahmedabad, beside the river Sabarmati, on the ruins of a pretty city called Karnawati, named after Karan Solanki, and Ashawal, named after the Bhil chieftain, Asha, one time leader of 600,000 tribals.

The Jhala king Satrasal's army had been defeated by Sultan Ahmed Shah's army led by Latif Khan in 1416AD, but did not lie still – they were involved in revolts, skirmishes and the battles of Kuva and Rankundal. The rulers of Idar and Nanded supported them in an unsuccessful attempt to overthrow the sultan. Realising that the Patdi-Kuva region, close to the capital of Ahmedabad, was not safe from the Muslims, especially as peaceful treaties signed by the sultans had served to transfer villages near Patdi to the Maleks of Dasada and to some Hindu chieftains, the capital of Zalawad was moved to Halwad, east of Patdi. But even this did not bring peace.

THE TOWERING PAVILION SURROUNDED BY COVERED GALLERIES IN THE COURTYARD OF THE HALWAD PALACE

FRONT VIEW OF THE HALWAD PALACE

REAR OF THE HALWAD PALACE SEEN FROM THE LAKESIDE WITH ITS ARRAY OF JAROKHAS

During one of the 16th century AD battles, Halwad was seized by the sultanate. According to the bards, it was restored at the request of the Hindu queen of the sultan; while others insist that the Jhalas attacked the sultan's camp by surprise, and forced him to return Halwad at the point of a sword! Yet another story tells us that the king of Halwad, Man Singh Jhala, became an outlaw and recaptured Halwad and the rest of Zalawad except for Viramgam and Mandal, to the west of Patdi.

The battlefield history of Halwad did not end with the fall of the sultanate and the emergence of the Mughals as the major national power in India. Over the centuries, the Jhala kingdom, which earlier had just two branches – the Patdi-Kuva Halwad and Limbdi dynasties – saw family feuds resulting in Zalawad's split into various states, including Wankaner and Wadhwan, which are described in other chapters of this book. Mughals took Halwad for some time in the 17th century AD, before Jaswant Sinhji got a sanad, or order, from Aurangzeb restoring Halwad to the former rulers. But insecurity did not end – the rulers of other Jhala Rajput states kept asserting their rights over Halwad, and the British, who had just proved their supremacy in India, disputed the claim of the eldest member of the clan over Halwad palace. Rai Sinhji, when he came to the throne of Halwad in 1730AD, took the prudent step of founding another city, Dhrangadhra, which became the capital of his descendants. Jaswant Sinhji moved the entire administration to Dhrangadhra in the late-18th century AD, though coronations and important occasions continued by tradition at the darbargadh of Halwad.

There was another skirmish between the Dhrangadhra ruler, Amar Sinhji, and his cousins at Wadhwan in 1805AD – curiously, over a goat! – but finally, in 1807-08AD, the Walker Settlement brought peace to Saurashtra, and the rulers could concentrate on administration and pursue other interests. One of the best rulers was HH Maharana Kanmai Sinhji, who was crowned in 1843AD. He

INTRICATELY CARVED WOODEN BRACKETS SUPPORT
THE COVERED GALLERIES AROUND THE COURTYARD
OF THE HALWAD PALACE. THE FAUNAL CARVINGS ON
THE BRACKETS ARE AMONG THE FINEST WOOD
SCULPTURES IN THE COUNTRY

EXQUISITE SCULPTURES AT THE SUNDER VILAS

was himself a Sanskrit, Persian and Gujarati scholar, and encouraged education. He introduced an English school in 1855AD, and commissioned many primary schools during his rule, and even a library. His good work was continued by his grandson, HH Maharana Ajit Sinhji, who in phases made primary and high school education free from 1907-09AD. HH Maharana Ajit Sinhji was a stickler for internal security – and it was he who started the Miana brigade to enforce law and order.

HH Maharana Ganshyam Sinhji, who succeeded HH Maharana Ajit Sinhji, became well known for opposing the British government's Salt Tax which kept the monopoly of salt trading with the British government, a piece of legislation which aroused antipathy in such measure that it gave birth to the greatest nationalist movement in India, a movement which ultimately broke the back of the Raj, starting with the Dandi march by Mahatma Gandhi.

The Little Rann of Kutch, just a few miles away, provided excellent revenue to the Dhrangadhra state, which stood to lose considerably by the Salt Tax. Permission was granted for Dhrangadhra state to trade with the eastern states like Bengal, but this

Dhrangadhra

ROYAL CHATTRIES AT THE HISTORIC CREMATION GROUNDS OF THE
JHALA RAJPUTS

ATTRACTIVE TILED FLOOR IN THE GALLERY AT THE ARSI VILAS

THE DARBARGADH OF DHRANGADHRA WHICH NOW HOUSES A SCHOOL AND
GOVERNMENT OFFICES. SOME ROOMS ARE BEING RENOVATED TO TAKE GUESTS

did not help much. HH Maharana Ganshyam Sinhji decided to start a chemical plant for salt related products in 1926AD. The salt industry he established employs around 2,500 people today, and has made the Little Rann of Kutch India's largest inland salt producer.

HH Maharana Mayurdhwaj Sinhji Megarajji the third, the present owner of the palaces of Dhrangadhra, came to the throne on 4th February 1942AD while he was still in his teens, and proved to be one of the most progressive rulers of Dhrangadhra. He had studied at Oxford, researched Vedic scriptures for his thesis, and learnt administration under the Gaekwads at Baroda. He took up causes like rural improvement, abolition of child marriages, compulsory education and women's right to property, and introduced acts related to marriages and divorces. He segregated executive administration from the judiciary. In 1947-48AD, he was involved in the integration of princely states into the Indian Union, and is one of the few royals alive who actually ruled before the merger of states. Today, he is working on researching various subjects, including the history of his clan in Zalawad. He has three sons. One is a Professor at Temple University in USA; the second deals with textiles in Maharashtra and occasionally exports garments; and the third, Yuvraj Sidhraj Sinhji, has the closest ties with Dhrangadhra – he has set up silversmith and stone carving workshops in the precincts of the

GALLERIES OVERLOOKING THE COURTYARD, ARSI VILAS

palace, often going there to handle affairs.

His silver furniture and marble carving are well known – besides finding a niche market in the metro-cities of India, they are exported overseas. His wife continues the family legacy of education. A part of the City palace has been converted into an English school, run by an enthusiastic lady executive

principal, with the family itself taking an interest in educating the children, and with Yuvraj Sidhraj Sinhji himself giving lectures. "My father, though only seventeen when he came to the throne, was a great administrator, and we were only a decade or two behind great states like Baroda where subjects like child marriage, untouchability and women's rights were concerned," Yuvraj Sidhraj Sinhji explains. "The palaces of Dhrangadhra are not as well maintained as some others in Gujarat, as we have not lived here for a very long time. We are working to restore some parts of the palace, though we have no plans to open them to tourists. At the city palace, where we have made the school, we may make available some rooms for tourists and business visitors to Dhrangadhra. The palace at Halwad, thirty kilometres from here towards Bhuj, is certainly the most beautiful of the palaces owned by our family, and we are planning a tourist complex there. We are restoring the palace, making a ten room hotel, and introducing motel facilities for passengers en route to Bhuj."

The Halwad palace, called rajmahal or darbargadh locally, was probably founded in the late-15th century AD as the fort of the Jhala Rajputs when they moved capital from Patdi to Halwad. Most of the medieval walls are now ruins, and the parts that are extant probably date from the 17th century AD. The front elevation as you enter through impressive gates shows walls encrusted with

A ROYAL HUNTING TENT, DISPLAYED AT THE ARSI VILAS

HORSES ARE A PASSION OF YUVRAJ SIDHRAJ SINHJI'S DAUGHTER. THEY GRAZE OUTSIDE THE SUNDER VILAS, THE ZANANA OF THE DHRANGADHRA PALACE

ornamental carved jarokha balconies, above a carved wooden door. The western wing was the zanana, easily distinguished by the intricate fretwork screens on the projecting balcony windows. Through these latticed screens, women looked down on comings-and-goings and could witness events in the forecourt, without being seen themselves.

The centre courtyard is one of the grandest in scale in Gujarat, with a huge pool surrounded by two storeys of covered galleries supported by some exquisitely carved wooden brackets – perhaps the most intricate woodwork in Gujarat, most of them sculptured with a variety of faunistic designs. From

the heart of the pool rises an elaborate polygonal pavilion, soaring six storeys high, with ornate jarokha balconies spiralling upwards to give what must have been unparalleled views of the Zalawad countryside. The covered galleries offer access to a suite of rooms which are unfurnished and derelict.

Behind the palace is a lake, which must have protected the old fortifications from invaders, and offered pleasant views from royal chambers. Ducks, coots, herons and waders can be seen at the lake. The steps leading down to the reservoir are used by local women to wash their colourful attire, and there are some historic temples facing the lake. Seen from

the lakeside, the palace is a festival of sculptured stone balconies.

A short distance west from the palace, beyond the town with its busy marketplace and residential areas, is the cremation ground of the Jhala Rajput kings. Ornate cenotaphs, called chattries for their domed ceilings, have been raised in memory of the dynastic rulers. There are rows of funeral stones, or palias, the equivalent of hero stones or tombstones in Europe, carved with sun or moon emblems depicting the time of the event according to the Indian calendar which follows the patterns of the moon, and images of war heroes on horseback and

Dhrangadhra

brave women in chariots. Some of the stones have images of arms or handprints of women, showing the act of sati, during which widowed wives, and occasionally even mothers, concubines and maids immolated themselves on the warrior king's pyre. Besides warriors, the palias often commemorate deaths of gadvis, bharats and charans, who were bardic poets and worked as ambassadors between princely states.

When the administrative capital of the Jhalas of Halwad moved to Dhrangadhra, the first palace they built was the darbargadh, right in the middle of the city today. The palace is an impressive spectacle with huge cupolas, towers and parapets. The best view is from the courtyard in the centre – the wings around the court are embellished with Romanesque arches, carved jarokha balconies and pillars. Part of the palace now houses government offices, but a section has been retained by the family, where Yuvraj Sidhraj Sinhji and his wife run their school. Portraits of royalty herald one's entry into the school, and the courtyard is decorated with some really fine sculpture including a reclining statue of Lord Buddha and an exquisitely sculptured stone lion. The classrooms offer a pleasant atmosphere for education. "When Kuvarani sahiba suggested starting the school, the only private English speaking school in Dhrangadhra, few believed it would survive," explains the principal, "but now we have a reasonable number of students from various

THE ARSI VILAS, MARDANA WING OF THE DHRANGADHRA PALACE COMPLEX IN THE TYPICAL VENETIAN-GOTHIC STYLE WITH DOMES AND POINTED ARCHES

communities – including Bharwad shepherds and goat herders – to learn primary English. Many of them, who feel they cannot cope with English at high school level, move to the neighbouring Gujarati medium school."

The royal family now resides in the new palace, probably built around the beginning of the 20th century AD, which is a massive and attractive palace set near a lake on the outskirts of Dhrangadhra. The entrance to the palace was through formal gardens, which, though still reflecting the original landscaping pattern, are no longer as well tended as in the days before the family moved to Maharashtra, and indeed no longer serve as entrance, the visitor entering the palace from the western gate. The zanana of the palace, called the Sunder vilas, and the mardana for men, called the Arsi vilas, are, like most other palaces of Gujarat, a blend of the Indian and European – carved Rajput jarokhas, sharing the same mural style with European arches and Italian pillars,

RECLINING SCULPTURE IN THE COURTYARD OF THE SCHOOL IN THE DARBARGADH

INTRICATE DEVOTIONAL SCULPTURE CARVED IN RELIEF AT THE ARSI VILAS

DETAIL OF INTRICATE CARVED WOODEN BRACKET IN THE COURTYARD OF THE HALWAD PALACE

while Gothic arches frame detailed carvings of Hindu gods, goddesses and friezes from the Ramayana, Mahabharata and other Hindu epics. Occasional winged angels tend to give the palace an Italian air. Courtyards and arcades connect or separate various wings of the palace, and throughout there are deep, attractively tiled galleries, with classical columns and arches, sometimes crowned by panelled ceilings. The family actually lives in the zanana, where Yuvraj Sidhraj Sinhji also has his offices with computers and other modern facilities, all rather in contrast to the historic architecture of the palace.

The darbarhall is now empty and unfurnished, but its sheer size, and the balconies upstairs which overlooked events below, give an insight into the past glory of this hall of audiences.

The Arsi vilas has the drawing room where the family entertains guests. It has a fabulous, decorated high ceiling, delicately carved, moulded, painted and gilded. Ornamental chandeliers and powerful old fans hang from the ceiling, carefully placed in the centre of oval contours. Carved stone balconies offer views of the hall from the first floor. A stuffed lion stands in a corner of the hall, while the mounted head of a huge sambhar deer hangs from another

wall. Portraits and paintings decorate this hall and the neighbouring rooms. A beautiful temple shrine stands in one of them. An exquisite embroidered hunting tent is the centrepiece in another of the rooms, which is furnished in oriental style, with chairs, tables, cabinets, decoration and frames for paintings, all of them made from wood carved in the finest detail and painted in bright colours.

In the grounds of the palace, you can see the family cars, including an old Studebaker, in the porticos; horses, which are a passion of one of the nine granddaughters of HH Maharana Mayurdhwaj Sinhji Megarajji the third; and outhouses, where artisans can be seen at work, making silver furniture and carving marble. The palace is not in the kind of condition you would expect from a princely state as important as Dhrangadhra, but it is nonetheless most impressive.

The Princely State of Gondal

11 GUN SALUTE STATE

NAULAKHA PALACE OF GONDAL

The royal family of Gondal belongs to the Jadeja Rajput clan, which claimed descent from Lord Krishna. Ardoi, near Gondal, was inherited by Mota Kumbhoji in the 16th century AD as his share of the states of Nawanagar (Jamnagar) and Rajkot, and at that time comprised just twenty villages. The state was extended by his son, Sagram Sinhji, who came to the throne in the 17th century AD, by conquests and valuable assistance from the subhedars of Junagadh. He made Gondal his capital and received Dhoraji and eighty six villages. His successor, Haloji, acquired Bhayavadar, and was succeeded by Kumbhoji the second, who became a major power in Kathiawad, both as a warrior and a diplomat. Despite being in the heart of the Kathiawadi peninsula, surrounded by major powers like Nawanagar (Jamnagar), Sardhar (Rajkot), Porbandar and Junagadh, he strengthened his kingdom and fortified towns like Gondal and Dhoraji. After Kumbhoji the second's death, there were turbulent times for his successors, with skirmishes with other rulers of Saurashtra, until the East India Company brought the region under control.

A certain Devoji, who came to the throne because one of the rulers did not have a son, helped Colonel Walker with the making of settlements circa 1807AD. Administration improved under Bhanabhai, a successor of Devoji, whose minister, diwan Durlabhai Buch, was an excellent administrator in the mid-19th century AD. But the golden period for Gondal began under Thakore Saheb Sagram Sinhji, who introduced schools and other infrastructural facilities. His son, HH Maharajah Bhagwat Sinhji, born in 1865AD, succeeded him as a minor in 1869AD. As was the practice in this situation, British

THE ENTRANCE TO THE NAULAKHA PALACE IS THROUGH THE ARCHWAY OF THE CLOCK TOWER

agents were appointed to handle affairs until the yuvraj was old enough to take the throne.

He was sent away to be educated, obtaining a Doctorate each in Medicine (Edinburgh) and Civil Law (Oxford). These qualifications he put to good use when he became ruler. He was a notable product of a British education, a bright boy who, in the words of his principal, "had advanced so far beyond his fellow students, that he had to be put in a class by himself." In order to give the finishing touches to his education, he undertook a tour of Europe under the guidance of Colonel Hancock. In 1883AD, he published his experiences in a book which was favourably received for its style, literary merit and fair and independent observations of its royal author. It was rare in this period for a ruler to take to literary work, though prior to this, and subsequently, a number of maharajahs did so.

He proved to be one of the 'model rulers' of India, who believed that simplicity was the path to progress. During his rule, no grand palaces were built, just extensions to existing palaces, mansions and bungalows. Rather, he invested in hospitals, schools for boys and girls, irrigation networks, sanitary drainage, underground electricity, telephone links and other public services. Proper tar and concrete roads were laid in the four towns and 175 villages of Gondal state. The highways had milestones, trees were numbered, tree felling was illegalised, a number of taxes and licence fees were abolished, education was free and compulsory, and private enterprise was encouraged. A principal source of revenue was railways, and rail links between the ports and the hinterland were set up in partnership with coastal states like Porbandar and Bhavnagar. Money was wisely invested in securities and businesses. Thanks to his insight, his heir HH Maharajah Bhojrajji, who succeeded him and who finally signed the Act of Accession, had one of the highest cash balances in Saurashtra – higher than many states with larger surface areas and higher revenues.

The oldest palace in Gondal is the darbargadh or Naulakha palace. It first had historic mention in 1748AD, though the family believes it was an

NAULAKHA PALACE WITH HIGHLY ORNATE 17TH CENTURY AD SCULPTURED STONE FACADE IN THE TYPICAL GUJARATI STYLE

Gondal

GOLD AND SILVER CASKETS USED FOR CARRYING MESSAGES FOR HH MAHARAJAH BHAGWAT SINHJI ON IMPORTANT OCCASIONS

ORCHARD PALACE, THE PERSONAL GUEST WING OF THE MAHARAJAH FOR VISITING ROYALTY AND GUESTS

DRAWING ROOM AT HUZOOR PALACE REFLECTS HH MAHARAJAH BHAGWAT SINHJI'S LOVE FOR EVERYTHING FRENCH

extension to an older fort. The palace is an absolute festival of intricate stone sculpture, with a superbly sculptured facade. The entrance is by a cusped archway crowned by a tall clock tower, and a courtyard with an old wing features devotional and other sculpture together with fine pillars. To the rear of the wing is the zanana, where the women from the royal family stayed in seclusion before Gondal became a progressive state in which women were no longer segregated, and this is easily distinguished by the exquisite fretwork balconies and intricate maze of tracery, through which the women could watch comings-and-goings in the courtyard without being observed. The old stables, with a profusion of pillars, still house horse drawn carriages, including a Shetland pony carriage and Victorian buggies, though not in immaculate condition – there are plans to restore the zanana and carriages.

The main palace has an impressive staircase lined with European style lampposts, leading to a courtyard of perhaps the grandest scale in Saurashtra's architectural annals. The courtyard is enclosed by richly carved pillars, meeting in equally attractive carved arches on all sides. Behind one of the rows of pillars is a pavilion where locals would wait for an audience with the ruler. It is easy to imagine that it was also used to witness dances and concerts in the open court. To the north are the old living quarters, still appointed with old brass four-posters, antique wooden furniture, brassware and

royal portraits. A fabulous linen chest stands in a corner of a corridor offering access to the rooms.

The row of pillars here form quite a spectacle with their fabulous toranas. The doors of the rooms are inlaid with brass and crowned by devotional sculpture. A spiral staircase, probably hewn from a single stone as it has no special support, leads to the upper storey.

Above this typically Indian section of the palace, the facade of the darbarhall, which was a later addition, has Venetian-Gothic arches and busts in the Egyptian style which seem to have been inspired by the ruler's visit to ancient civilisation sites in that country. The darbarhall is appointed with gilt wooden chairs, making no secret of HH Maharajah Bhagwat Sinhji's obsession with 19th century AD France, a love that led to his modelling Gondal on the lines of Paris and other European cities. The two rows of chairs on a carpeted floor lead to a gilt throne. Two antique mirrors stand on either side of the hall. The walls are punctuated by huge windows, and lined with a row of limestone carving. Four stuffed panthers in mid-snarl threaten from the corners. A huge chandelier, one of many that hang from the ceiling, still illuminates the hall. Beside the hall is the casket room with a variety of caskets in silver and gold, which carried gifts and messages for HH Maharajah Bhagwat Sinhji on his silver anniversary as ruler of Gondal, on his 61st birthday and on his golden jubilee. An interesting pair of

19TH CENTURY AD FRENCH GILT CHAIRS IN THE DARBARHALL OF THE NAULAKHA PALACE

Sinhji, the present owner of the palace, loves motor cars, and this is evident in the models of cars here, including some in cut crystal. Next door is the dining hall, with an exaggerated arch in the centre, a carved, mirror topped dining table, heavy wooden side tables, cabinets lined with an assortment of objects in sterling silver, porcelain and crystal, and a pair of Ming vases by the door. A massive chandelier illuminates the room.

The highlight of the palace is the library. Still in original condition, books on various subjects, illustrating the intellectual merits of HH Maharajah Bhagwat Sinhji line the mahogany cabinets; charcoal drawings of him and his wife hang from the wall, and the fabulous carved writing table, with the ruler's plush chair and some smaller chairs arranged

THE LIBRARY AT THE HUZOOR PALACE

weighing scales, on which he was measured against food grains, sometimes finished in silver or gold, depending on the importance of the occasion, stands in another room. The palace is lined with finely carved jarokha balconies, some of them with unusual canopies resembling leaping lions, and exquisitely hewn brackets.

British agents, appointed to handle the affairs of Gondal while HH Maharajah Bhagwat Sinhji was a minor, built the residency, a large bungalow, which HH Maharajah Bhagwat Sinhji extended into the Huzoor palace, with three wings surrounding a courtyard garden with porticos in front and rear, set in acres of fruit orchards and informal gardens. The drawing room again reflects HH Maharajah Bhagwat Sinhji's love for everything French – gilt wooden settees and chairs in Louis XIV style, crystal from Europe, royal portraits, pleasant rugs and objets d' art. One clock here is said to be a replica of one in the Victoria and Albert museum in London. His great-great-grandson, HH Maharajah Jyotendar

INTERESTING DEEP CARVED EMBELLISHMENTS IN STONE AT THE NAULAKHA PALACE

in a semi-circle in front, provide the office space from which he controlled Gondal. Behind the desk are further chairs brought here from his various visits to the Delhi darbar. The Maharajah's ageing servant, who now looks after hotel guests in the Orchard palace, recalls the times under this great man's rule when Gondal was a garden city of which its citizens were proud, a city monitored personally by the man himself. He recalls HH Maharajah Bhagwat Sinhji working regularly late into the night, then taking an inspection tour of the city before retiring.

On the upper storey are the royal apartments, connected by an old lift. A gallery from the palace leads to the Orchard wing, which once housed guests, but is now an Heritage Hotel.

HH Maharajah Jyotendar Sinhji's love of cars has induced him to maintain his ancestral collection of vintage and classic cars: these include HH Maharajah Bhagwat Sinhji's 1910AD New Engine, and European cars from the 1920s and 1930s AD including a Daimler, a Delage and a Mercedes; a fleet of imposing American cars, with a 1935AD Packard 2-door convertible coupe, Fords, Buicks, Cadillacs from 1941AD and 1947AD, a Studebaker, a 1950s AD Cadillac limousine, and Chevrolets – a particular favourite of HH Bhojrajji and HH Vikram Sinhji; 4-wheel drive vehicles that have seen many royal hunts; and sports cars like the Jaguar XK150, Mercedes 300SL and Surtees formula 5000 of the 1950s AD raced by HH Maharajah Jyotendar Sinhji

and his bother at many motor sport events and to memorable victories.

Yuvraj Himanshu Sinh shares his father's love of fast cars and drives a Corvette ZR-1, a Chevrolet Camaro and a Mercedes. Two of the railway carriages, in which the maharajahs travelled, can still be seen in the palace confines. One of them is resplendent with a suite comprising dining room, drawing room, bedroom, bathroom and kitchen,

and has been restored for guests of the Heritage Hotel wing. The other, still in original condition, stands in the saloon house, from where tracks led to the railway station for the saloon to be hitched up to regular trains until the 1960s AD! Both the saloons are beautifully finished, with inlaid wood panelling, historic photographs and crystal light fixtures.

One kilometre from the palace is the Riverside palace, a good sized bungalow built in the 1880s AD

ROYAL APARTMENTS AT THE HUZOOR PALACE

SAGRAM SINHJI HIGH SCHOOL, BUILT IN THE 1920S AD, SO CLOSELY MODELLED ON ETON COLLEGE WITH ITS GOTHIC ARCHES AND CLOCK TOWER, THAT LITIGATION TOOK PLACE AGAINST THE STATE

Gondal

THE PAVILION AT THE NAULAKHA PALACE, WHERE SUBJECTS WAITED FOR AN AUDIENCE WITH THEIR KING

ONE OF THE PRESENT MAHARAJAH'S RECENT ACQUISITIONS FOR HIS COLLECTION AT THE HUZOOR PALACE

as the mansion residence of the crown prince, but now an Heritage Hotel, with shade giving trees and gardens. The palace is entered by a European style living room, appointed with an old cabinet, English prints, oil paintings, settees and a carved table, and illuminated by a massive chandelier brought here from the darbarhall of the Naulakha palace. The galleries are lined with deer trophies, prints, paintings and historic photographs of HH Maharajah Bhagwat Sinhji and other ancestors, of HH Maharajah Jyotendar Sinhji, and of the late Kumar Shree Dharam Kumar Sinhji of Bhavnagar, father of Maharani Kumud Kumari.

The rooms are furnished in French country and Victorian styles with four-poster beds, old dressers, oil paintings, fitted carpets, crystal light fittings and original fans. In contrast to the European ambience of the palace, the family has made an Indian room for visitors to absorb some local flavour, and this is decorated with Kathiawadi beadwork embroideries, wall hangings, miniature paintings, devotional pictures and brass utensils.

A short walk down the road is the Sagram Sinhji High School, built during HH Maharajah Bhagwat Sinhji's rule, an imposing building in the Gothic style modelled along the lines of Eton, with arches and a clock tower. The school was built to educate Rajput boys, and to train them to be administrators, but in the 1930s AD, during the golden jubilee celebrations of HH Maharajah Bhagwat Sinhji, it was declared open to all. The school is now a municipal educational institution, and poorly maintained, but is worth a visit for its intricate wooden ceilings and Italian marble floors – a contrast to the simple flooring of the palaces, reflecting the greatness of HH Maharajah Bhagwat Sinhji, who spent more on public welfare buildings than on his own residences.

Forty-nine kilometres south of Gondal, Dhoraji, the second capital of Gondal state, has a magnificent palace, the darbargadh, now an archaelogical monument. The palace is a marvellous work of stone sculpture and architecture with lovely fretwork windows, carved jarokha balconies and intricate arches. Dhoraji has an impressive railway station and towers, and was an important outpost on the railway trade routes in HH Maharajah Bhagwat Sinhji's time. Upleta, the third most important town in

CARVED JAROKHA AT THE NAULAKHA PALACE

THE RICH FACADE OF DHORAJI PALACE

HH MAHARAHJAH JYOTENDAR SINHJI, MAHARANI
KUMUD KUMARI AND YUVRANI HEMA KUMARI
SINH, AT THE HUZOOR PALACE

Gondal state, has a darbargadh with projecting balconies overlooking a river, and bastioned walls on its banks.

The present family is enterprising and has not rested on its laurels. HH Maharajah Jyotendar Sinhji, Maharani Kumud Kumari and Yuvraj Himanshu Sinh are involved in businesses, investments, real estate, construction and even small enterprises in Bombay, Gondal, Rajkot, Delhi and the United Kingdom. They have converted two properties into Heritage Hotels, and plan to renovate their palatial mansion in Bangalore into an hotel.

The family's lifestyle blends east and west. Their meals are often European, but during religious festivals they eat only Gujarati food. They celebrate Navrati, with dances in the Naulakha palace, Diwali with their elder clan in Kutch in traditional style, and Christmas in Bombay or Gondal in the English style. House parties during festivals can last for a week, with friends and relatives invited from all over India and beyond. The youngsters enjoy treasure hunts, car racing, squash and riding, while the elders relax in the drawing rooms or rock gardens. Picnics by the lakeshore and camping in the family's private grounds are always enjoyed.

The Princely State of Nawanagar (Jamnagar)

13 GUN SALUTE STATE

Historically called Nawanagar, or 'the new city', Jamnagar was one of the most important princely states of Saurashtra. The city today is called Jamnagar or the city of Jams, after the hereditary title held by the rulers of Nawanagar from the time of Jam Saheb Rawal, who founded the city in 1540AD.

In the 16th century AD, Jam Saheb Rawal believed that his father, Rao Lakho, the ruler of many fiefdoms in Kutch and a famous warrior in the court of the sultan, had been killed by the Lakhiavara branch of his own clan: a claim denied by the bards of the Maharaos of Kutch, who belong to the Lakhiavara branch. Jam Saheb Rawal decided to take revenge on the Lakhiavara family. Hamir, the head of this branch, was killed, but his sons, Khengar and Sahib, escaped to Ahmedabad to seek an audience with Sultan Muhammad Bhegada, who, they hoped, would settle their disputes. After a long and arduous journey, they reached Ahmedabad, but Jam Saheb Rawal had already become an important vassal of the sultan, and they had few hopes of getting a hearing.

Khengar and Sahib became capable horsemen

and on one occasion joined the sultan's hunting party as royal retainers. As luck would have it, the sultan was attacked by a lion, and the two Rajput youths

STATUE OF JAM SAHEB RANJIT SINHJI

saved his life. The sultan agreed to invade and take the fiefdoms from Jam Saheb Rawal. Jam Saheb Rawal got ready for battle. He was not afraid of taking on the mighty armies of the sultan, say the bards, but in a dream was cautioned by Ashapura mata, the mother goddess of the Jadeja clan, to move to Kathiawad, where, she promised, he would be a powerful ruler.

Jam Saheb Rawal left for the peninsula, with a contingent so large that, as the bards record, "the earth at the tramp of the army began to tremble and the dust from it hid the heavens from Jadeja eyes", and immediately invaded the territories of the Chavdas, Dedas, Jethwas and Wadhels, taking over important villages like Jodhia, Ghumali, Nagnath port and· Khambalia. He defeated Jam Saheb Tamachi to take over Dhrol, and contrived to kill a Jethwa king to win important coastal trade posts. The Jethwa princes, thirsty for revenge, joined forces with the Wadhels and Walas (Kathi darbar rulers) to take back their territories, and to discourage further incursions by Jam Saheb Rawal.

The troops harnessed by Jam Saheb Rawal were large enough to repel the invaders, but the artillery was weak. Jam Saheb Rawal's troops were unable to

Jamnagar

KHAMBALIYA GATE, ONE OF THE FIVE IMPRESSIVE WHITE STONE GATES OF JAMNAGAR

the arrogant Vaghela chieftain, immediately harnessing his troops and marching on the Vaghela, destroying their city after a long battle.

Jam Saheb Rawal died in 1562AD and was succeeded by Jam Saheb Vibhoji, who helped the Jhala princes take back their capital of Halwad from usurpers. He was succeeded in 1569AD by Sataji, who was the contemporary of Sultan Muzaffar Shah of Gujarat, a weak ruler. Sataji declared the state independent and even coined his own currency. During his rule, the Mughals attacked Junagadh and tried to relieve the Ghori Muslims of the fort. The Jadejas supported the Ghoris and the mighty Mughal armies had to retreat before the allied forces of Junagadh and Nawanagar. In return for this, the Jam clan was awarded territories by the Ghoris of Junagadh. But the sultanate of Gujarat was destroyed by the Mughals, and the sultan retreated to the Barda hills where the Jam ruler gave him sanctuary. The angry Mughals returned with stronger forces and at the battle of Bhucharmori in 1590AD, the greatest battle in the Kathiawadi peninsula, stormed Nawanagar. Sataji asked for peace, and got it, and much of his kingdom was restored, apart from some important areas which remained in Mughal hands until 1608AD. The clan's capital was moved to Khambaliya.

The rule of Jam Saheb Jasoji, who succeeded Sataji, passed peacefully, but Jam Saheb Jasoji's successor, Jam Saheb Lakhaji, who was actually his

withstand the cannon fire of the allies, and began to retreat. But loyal followers of Jam Saheb Rawal agreed to spike the cannon. During the battle, permission had been given for the women to meet each other, and, disguised as Jadeja women in heavy purdah and veiled palanquins, the warriors entered the enemy camp and blocked the cannon's vents. They were discovered and speared to death, but the cannon were no longer effective, and the invaders had to retreat.

Another story of Jam Saheb Rawal reveals the

important relationship between the ruler and the charans, gadvis and bhats, who were the bards, historians and diplomats of the Rajput royal families. Jam Saheb Rawal, who had been very pleased with one of the charans, had pledged always to support them. One day, the charans were on their way to meet a Vaghela chieftain. The charans were slighted by the Vaghela chieftain, and uttered a curse that his kingdom would be destroyed, whereupon they immediately committed suicide. When Jam Saheb Rawal heard of the incident, he set out to destroy

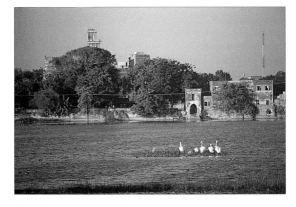

THE LAL PALACE OF JAMNAGAR BESIDE THE LAKE

ENTRANCE TO THE DARBARGADH

MORPAD FORT

nephew and who ruled from 1629-45AD, faced a serious invasion from Azam Khan, the subha of the Mughal emperor at Ahmedabad – this was, however, forestalled by the offering and acceptance of tributes. There is a story of how the Mughals agreed to give back the kingdom to Vibhaji, younger brother of Jam Saheb Lakhaji, but Vibhaji asked for a kingdom for his elder brother. The grateful Jam Saheb Lakhaji made the two sons of Vibhaji rulers of Sardhar (present-day Rajkot) and of Gondal. Another story tells us that after the invasions there was not enough money to install Jam Saheb Lakhaji on the throne – a Jain bania, Wadhwan Shah, came up with a loan of 30 lakh koris and gave Jam Saheb Lakhaji a coronation befitting an Indian prince. In the 1640s AD, Jam Saheb Lakhaji made an unsuccessful attempt at becoming independent from the Mughal emperors, but the revolt was crushed by Shah Jahan's forces in Gujarat.

His successor, Jam Saheb Ranmalji, say the bards, fell in love with a member of a mendicant's family, and was cursed by the mendicant that the wrong son would be his heir. Jam Saheb Ranmalji fell ill as a result of the curse, and his powerful queen, from the Rathore dynasty of Rajasthan, crowned her son Sataji as heir apparent of Nawanagar. Jam Saheb Ranmalji was aware that Sataji was not his son, but the son of a previous husband of the queen, but ill health prevented him from opposing the queen, who had a strong

following. He called on his two brothers to revolt against the crown prince. Internal feuds followed, and only the women were allowed to meet. Rai Sinhji, Jam Saheb Ranmalji's brother, and his loyal warriors, disguised in purdah, succeeded in dethroning Sataji. But Sataji appealed to the Mughal emperor for help and the Mughal governor's army rampaged Nawanagar and killed Rai Sinhji. Rai Sinhji's son, Tamachi, escaped from Nawanagar and made his hideout at Khambaliya and Okha, at the western tip of the peninsula, from where, from time to time, he was able to make surprise attacks on Nawanagar and its territories.

In due time, however, the Muslim Mughal empire began to fall into ruins, and the Hindu Marathas began to emerge as the strongest power in India. The Hindus looked upon Tamachi as the rightful heir to Nawanagar, and his exploits are part of many historic poems. Tamachi managed to recover Nawanagar after concluding a treaty with Jaswant Sinhji of Marwar, a man of important status at Ahmedabad, under which he would supply 1,000 infantry and 1,000 cavalry when required. Skirmishes did not end in the 18th century AD. There was war between Nawanagar and Morvi, and an invasion by the Mughal armies, led by Ajit Sinhji of Marwar, in an attempt to salvage their status as a national power.

In the 1740s AD, Jam Saheb Lakhaji was a weak ruler, and Meru Khwas, one of the slaves, became

Jamnagar

LAKOTA PALACE SEEN FROM JAMSAROVAR LAKE

towers and eight lesser gates.

Towards the end of the 18th century AD, Meru Khwas died, and Jam Saheb Jasoji made a settlement with his sons giving them three territories. During Jam Saheb Jasoji's rule there was a minor battle with the Kathis over a horse, and a mutiny at Kandorna fort which he settled by paying off the garrison and taking the fort. In 1807AD, the Walker Settlement brought peace between the various princely states of Kathiawad, but Nawanagar was still the centre of disputes. Jam Saheb Jasoji acknowledged the rights of his brother, Sataji, but did not give him his due portion, as he was addicted to opiates.

The golden period for Nawanagar began in the 1830s AD, when Jam Saheb Ranmalji came to the throne. He revamped the state systems, restored Dwarka, improved Nawanagar and, during the decade's famine, adopted drought relief measures ranging from the creation of reservoirs, including Jamsarovar lake, right in the heart of Nawanagar, to the building of Lakota palace and Kotha bastion to provide employment. He died in 1852AD, and one of his seven sons, Vibhaji, succeeded him.

Jam Saheb Vibhaji introduced a railway line to Rajkot, schools and medical facilities, and was awarded the honour of KCIE in 1876AD and a salute of fifteen guns in 1879AD. During his rule, there was a mutiny in 1857AD, when the Waghers of Okha rebelled. The Waghers were defeated by the Nawanagar forces led by Jhalam Sinhji, and the

dominant. The spirited queen, who could not bear the thought of being dominated by a slave, hired assassins in vain attempts to get rid of Meru Khwas. The nobles appealed for help to Rao Godji of Kutch, but even he could not overthrow Meru Khwas. Meru Khwas besieged Modhpur fort, where some members of the ruling family lived, and became ruler of Nawanagar. He conquered Jasdan from the Kathi darbar, Sur Vala Khaccher, who offered him Atkot and requested the return of his capital at Jasdan. To Meru Khwas' dismay, however, Atkot belonged not

to Sur Vala Khaccher, but to his cousin, Dadar Khaccher. Angry at being cheated by the Kathis, Meru Khwas declared war and the Kathis, though knowing that Nawanagar was more powerful, decided to die by the sword. Bardic poetry of Kathiawad is rich in tales of the brave Kathi warriors who went to war knowing their fate, but preferring death in battle to humiliation. With this victory, Meru Khwas became a powerful ruler and surrounded Nawanagar with a huge wall, with five impressive carved white stone gates, twenty-two

ENTRANCE TO THE DARBAGADH

SUNSET AT LAKOTA PALACE

grateful Jam Saheb Vibhaji gave Jhalam Sinhji's son, Umed Sinhji (Rai Sinhji), rule over many districts. As Jam Saheb Vibhaji had fourteen wives but no sons, Rai Sinhji was the potential heir to the throne. But Jam Saheb Vibhaji then married a Sindhi woman, who gave birth to Kaluba, a wild and savage youth. The Sindhi woman had Rai Sinhji murdered to pave the way for Kaluba to become the legal heir. In the event, Kaluba's violent behaviour made him an outlaw, and he was barred from succession. Instead, the throne went eventually to Ranjit Sinhji, who had been at Rajkumar College and later went to Cambridge in 1888AD with MacNaughten, later to become the principal of Rajkumar College. Ranjit Sinhji was an excellent cricketer, rivalling the best in

the world. He played county cricket for Sussex and test cricket for England. Neville Cardus called him 'the Prince of the Orient', wielding his bat like 'Houdini's wand'. In 1899AD he became the first batsman to score 3,000 runs in a single first class season, and on a single day he scored two double centuries for Sussex against Yorkshire.

The British government had tried to influence Jam Saheb Vibhaji to give the crown to Ranjit Sinhji rather than to Kaluba or Jaswant Sinhji, for after his years at Cambridge he was more to their liking and more of a 'pukka saheb'. But in 1903AD it was Jaswant Sinhji, Jam Saheb Vibhaji's rightful heir, who came to the throne. Jam Saheb Jaswant Sinhji's rule was shortlived, however, and he died of typhoid

in 1907AD.

Jam Saheb Ranjit Sinhji was duly installed as ruler on 7th March 1907AD. By then, all feuds, conflicts and battles had been settled, and he was able to set about the task of removing poverty from Nawanagar. Jam Saheb Ranjit Sinhji realised the importance of having a proper port to export the various agricultural and industrial products of Nawanagar, and so Bedi port was developed along the southern coast of the Gulf of Kutch. He made arrangements with the Gaekwad dynasty of Baroda, which had a port in Okhamandal, the north western tip of the peninsula, to use their dock facilities, and got their financial support for a railway link between Nawanagar and Okha, via Dwarka. Squalid slums

KOTHA BASTION OF JAMNAGAR

were replaced by modern housing, and sanitary drainage and a dispensary introduced. Free primary education was offered in 1911AD, secondary education in 1916AD, and the entire city was electrified in the 1920s AD.

Jam Saheb Ranjit Sinhji had four nephews: Pratap Sinhji, Digvijay Sinhji, Himmat Sinhji and Duleep Sinhji. Duleep Sinhji grew up to be a distinguished cricketer like his uncle, and indeed represented England. Jam Saheb Digvijay Sinhji inherited the title and throne from his uncle, and proved to be an able ruler. He represented India at the Imperial War conference. In 1942AD, the British government in Bombay would not give much assistance to a Polish ship that had escaped the unwelcome attention of German warships, and Jam

Saheb Digvijay Sinhji personally helped them land at Bedi port and gave them a refugee camp at Balachari, a fact acknowledged even today by the Polish government. In 1948AD, Jam Saheb Digvijay Sinhji signed the agreements merging Nawanagar state into the Indian Union. He was made governor of Saurashtra, a new state created by the Indian government to reflect linguistic practice, which was later merged into Bombay state in 1956AD, and still later, after the Mahagujarat agitation, into the state of Gujarat.

The old royal residence of the Jam sahebs is the darbargadh, a two storey palace probably built in the 1540s AD when Nawanagar was founded, but obviously extended over the next three or four centuries, as can be seen from the Venetian-Gothic

arches in some wings. The palace has some fine examples of stone carvings – fabulous carved jarokha balconies, curved arches, fretwork jali-screens, carved pillars and sculpture. The walls outside have carved jarokha balconies in the Indian tradition, a carved gate and Venetian-Gothic arches. The palace is now empty except for the guards. Across the road from the darbargadh, Willingdon Crescent was one of Jam Saheb Ranjit Sinhji's attempts to replace the choked slums of Nawanagar with a new citadel inspired by his European journeys. The crescent comprised arcades of cusped arches, larger on the ground floor and smaller on the upper storey, pilasters on the curving walls, and balusters on the parapet. Statues of the Jam sahebs stand in the centre. The royal emblem of the Jam saheb crowns the crescent.

Another of Jam Saheb Ranjit Sinhji's great European inspirations was the Pratap vilas palace, drawn from various Italian architectural styles, with Romanesque arches, Gothic arches, bay windows, classical columns, balustraded terraces, rounded stone porticos and a profusion of Italian marble – with some oriental style touches visible in the stone carvings, and in the zanana wing for the women of the royal family. Building on the palace began in 1907AD and was completed in 1915AD. The interiors have a profusion of large rooms, banqueting halls, drawing rooms, curving staircases and long, deep galleries. At the top of the building, the domed turrets have fabulous views of Jamnagar city. The darbarhall hosted badminton matches, royal banquets, grand parties and official functions. The walls are spanned by portraits of the Jam sahebs, cricketing photographs and paintings, a portrait of W G Grace with Ranjit Sinhji, and oil paintings by Burne Jones, Stuart Lloyd and E Long.

An older palace in Nawanagar was the Lakota palace, built as a drought relief measure by Jam Saheb Ranmalji on an island in the centre of the lake, known as the Ranmal or Jamsarovar sanctuary, where birds flock in vast numbers. The palace is rather like a fort, with semi-circular bastions, turrets, carved jarokha balconies, a pavilion with extensive views and guard-rooms housing swords, powder flasks and musket loops. Stone bridges lead to the palace. Inside you can see frescos on the walls, most

of them depicting the Jam sahebs on horseback shooting lions, pigsticking or holding court, but some showing Indian lifestyles like the picturesque holy bathing ghats at Dwarka, one of the most important pilgrimage sites for Hindus.

Beautiful domed pavilions face the palace from the embankments of the lake. The massive Kotha bastion rises up from the side of the lake, with its parapet offering panoramic views on every side. This

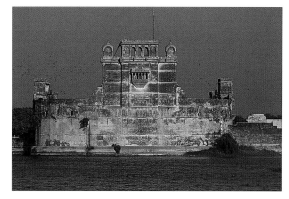

LAKOTA PALACE RESEMBLES A FORT

would have provided a good defence measure, as the Jam sahebs were involved in skirmishes even after the Walker Settlement brought British peace to Saurashtra.

The rooms in the Lakota palace once offered accommodation to important guests of the Jam sahebs, but this was later replaced by the Lal palace, built in reddish stone and now used as a government guesthouse.

In 1966AD, Shatrushailya Sinhji inherited the properties and title of Jam saheb. He also inherited

the family's love of cricket, and represented Saurashtra in first class cricket. He is acknowledged by locals as an expert at judging gems and jewellery. His main enthusiasm, though, is wildlife. He is the convenor of the Sir Peter Scott Institute for Nature which undertakes various research projects in Saurashtra, often with foreign collaboration. He has converted the palace grounds into a preserve for antelope, birds, reptiles and smaller mammals. Blackbuck antelope, including white mutants, blue bull antelope, porcupine, Indian hare, monitor lizard, grey francolin and other wildlife roam freely in the vast acreage of the palace grounds. Crocodile, brought in from nearby reservoirs during the drought, are enclosed here. The menagerie includes African crowned crane, bred here in captivity. The investment in the project was about Rs.30 lakhs (3 million Rupees), an enormous sum by Indian living standards. Jam Saheb Shatrushailya Sinhji is now campaigning for a number of further causes in this region. Harshad Kumari Sharma, also of the Jamnagar royal family, is prominent amongst monument conservationists, and one of the senior members of INTACH, an Indian heritage trust.

Outside Jamnagar, and now a military school, the Balachari palace is an eagle eyried Morpad fort by the sea, which often features in the history of Nawanagar and Porbandar and still looks formidable; and the Kileshwar summer palace, on a peak on Barda hill, is now a school.

The Princely State of Jasdan

NON-SALUTE STATE

The Kathi darbars were the traditional rulers of Kutch and Saurashtra, and the tales of their valour are legion. The medieval period saw a series of fresh invasions into Gujarat. Arab incursions into Sindh forced some chieftains from the Jadeja and Jhala Rajput clans to move into Kutch and Saurashtra. The turbulent middle ages at Rajasthan saw members of Rajput clans like the Gohils pushed towards Bhavnagar and the Afghan dynasty of Jalore find a new capital at Palanpur; and, in the 15th century AD, Muslim sultans became the major power in Gujarat. The Mughals conquered Gujarat in the 16th century AD, and the Marathas rose to power in the 17th and 18th centuries AD in the hills of southern Gujarat. The Kathis were pushed into the hinterland of Kathiawad, where they ruled over states like Jasdan, Jetpur and Bhilka, while the more powerful invaders took the ports. Yet the Kathis did not give in, and many were the battles they fought with the Rajputs, often putting their powerful neighbours to flight. "The Catti still adores the sun," wrote Colonel Tod in *Annal and Antiquities of Rajasthan*, "scorns the peaceful arts and is much less contented with the tranquil subsistence of industry than the precarious earnings of his former predatory pursuit."

One of the most important Kathi rulers during British rule was Darbar Saheb Ala Khaccher of Jasdan. He brought in a strong system of internal security to the crime ravaged heartlands, and introduced numerous reforms. A flamboyant character, he endowed the small state of Jasdan with fine architecture and facilities. A great sportsman, Darbar Saheb Ala Khaccher played two hours of lawn tennis daily, and Jasdan palace was one of the first to have tennis courts. He was also a good cricketer and polo player, and fond of breeding high quality horses.

Darbar Saheb Shivraj Kumar Khaccher was another distinguished member of the Jasdan dynasty. His expertise was natural history, and during his lifetime the Hingolgadh forests that had protected the fort of the darbar sahebs of Jasdan and later provided his ancestors with game, was declared a wildlife sanctuary. Where his ancestors had organised duck shoots, Darbar Saheb Shivraj Kumar Khaccher introduced nature conservation education camps for school children with the help of his cousin, Lav

HINGOLGADH CASTLE

CANNON AT HINGOLGADH CASTLE

Jasdan

Anant vilas palace, showing ornate balconies in European and Indian styles

Jasdan

JAROKHA BALCONIES AT HINGOLGADH CASTLE

GALLERY WITH TILED FLOOR AT THE HINGOLGADH CASTLE

Kumar, and invited ornithologists like Salim Ali for bird ringing study projects in Hingolgadh sanctuary. Darbar Saheb Shivraj Kumar Khaccher also represented India in international conservation workshops and seminars.

His son, Darbar Saheb Satyajit Kumar Khaccher, shares his family's love of horses and livestock. He breeds cattle and horses at his stud farm, exports cattle products, and maintains pets like pedigree dogs, purebred pigeons and exotic birds. "We have

converted the Hingolgadh castle into an Heritage Hotel," explains his mother, Rajmata of Jasdan, "but our focus is on quality groups. We take only selected tourists."

The Hingolgadh castle was built in 1665AD on a site where the Bayodra fort had been demolished by the Rajput rulers of Junagadh. The castle is approached through scrubland, and stands proud atop a forested hill about 1,000 feet above sea level, in the heart of the six and a half square kilometre

Hingolgadh wildlife sanctuary, and features semi-circular bastions, imposing walls and a facade of ornately carved jarokha balconies and galleries. The European style ramparts are guarded by cannon, inscriptions dating their casting to the 1700s AD. In the centre of the castle is a pleasantly open courtyard, filled with shady trees and European lampposts.

A spiral staircase leads up to a gallery, which in turn offers access to the dining hall, bedrooms and

BALCONIES AT THE ANANT VILAS PALACE

further flights of stairs. The rooms are quaintly old fashioned, with four-poster beds made from brass, wrought iron or carved wood, and intricate wooden furniture and English baths complete the scene. The galleries are beautifully floored with colourful European tiles or marble, and windows bring in views that are nothing short of magnificent. Indian gazelle, blue bull antelope and other wildlife roam the area, and are often seen from the windows. The drawing room is furnished with brightly upholstered settees, wrought iron chandeliers and oil paintings of landscapes and horses.

The family lives by a small rivulet in the Anant vilas palace within the old darbargadh, with archways and winding paths leading into the palace. The front elevation shows ornate balconies drawn from Indian and European styles, classical columns and Venetian-Gothic arches, with the wings of the palace surrounding a fountained courtyard garden. An highlight of the palace is the imposing, classical balustraded staircase. The substantial library houses a variety of books in mahogany cabinets, and the family has a good collection of Kathiawadi beadwork, embroidered textiles, brass utensils and local antiques.

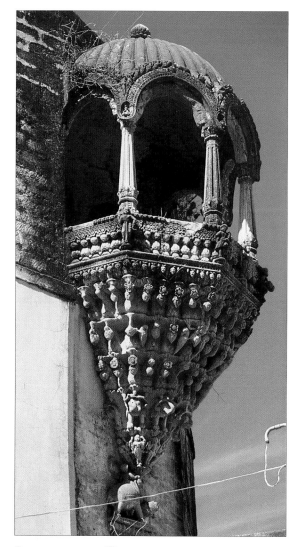

JAROKHA AT THE HINGOLGADH CASTLE

The Princely State of Junagadh

**13 GUN
SALUTE STATE**

ONE OF THE FAMOUS CRESCENT GATES OF THE CITY
OF JUNAGADH

The princely state of Junagadh at the southern tip of the Kathiawadi peninsula, now better known as Saurashtra, comprises picturesque hills and coastal areas with historic ports and harbours. This region owed its prosperity to overseas trade from the west, to fertile fields that received rains from the south west monsoon breezes, and to grassland that could be harvested for cattle and other ethnic livestock. The renowned Gir cattle known for their milk production, together with the Kathiawadi horses, rated among the best in the subcontinent for riding, and the superb natural defences of rocks and hills, combined to make Junagadh one of the most coveted seats of power for many years. Archaeological finds indicate that civilisation existed here in the third millennium BC, and coins from the Alexander the Great period, 3rd to 5th centuries AD, have been found in the hills of Junagadh. In even clearer historic perspective, the powerful Mauryan emperors, who, from Patna in eastern India, ruled over a massive region from Kabul in present-day Afghanistan and the Kashmir valley of the western Himalayas to the Deccan plateau in southern India from the 4th century BC to the 4th century AD, had an important western outpost at Junagadh.

In the 3rd century BC, Emperor Ashoka was shocked at the sufferings of battle inflicted by his army during the victorious conquest of Kalinga. He took solace in the non-violent preaching of Buddhism, and spread this through missions to various kingdoms of south east Asia, inscribing edicts on rocks for people to follow at four different sights in India, one of which was Junagadh. Buddhist monastic caves of the Mauryan dynastic period can be seen in the rocks of Junagadh. The 150BC inscriptions of his descendant, Rudraman, attests that the Saurashtra peninsula was indeed an important province of the Mauryan kingdom, with Junagadh as one of its important centres. With the decline of the Mauryans and the rise of the Guptas, another Aryan dynasty, as a major national force, Junagadh continued to be an important centre of power in the western reaches of the Indian peninsula up to the middle of the 6th century AD.

For some centuries, it is said, Junagadh was abandoned and the fort fell into ruin, only to be found and restored by the Chudasama Rajputs, who

Junagadh

made it their capital between the 9th and 15th centuries AD. During this period, it is said, the fort saw sixteen battles and sieges, including a twelve-year long battle over a princess. Eventually the king was slain in battle and the fort conquered, but to no avail, for the hapless woman opted to commit suicide!

Finally, like the rest of Gujarat, Junagadh fell to Muslim invasion in the 1470s AD when Sultan Muhammad Bhegada took the fort after a long siege. The sultan had his capital at Ahmedabad, and did not have much interest in staying in Junagadh.

He tried to build mosques in the fort, which were never completed: even an attempt at converting the Rank Devi palace – built in memory of a queen by a member of the Chudasama Rajput dynasty – into a mosque for Friday services, did not succeed. The Mughals took Junagadh from the Gujarat sultanate and thenceforward ruled through their subhedars appointed to handle the Kathiawadi peninsula. Custody of Junagadh was given to the descendants of Adil Shah, a great warrior from Ghor province in Afghanistan, who had accompanied the Mughal emperor Humayun as he took over of Delhi in the

THE DARBARHALL OF THE CITY PALACE OF JUNAGADH, NOW A MUSEUM DISPLAYING SILVER-PLATED CHAIRS AND THRONE

THE 18TH CENTURY AD ROYAL MAQBARA OF THE NAWABS OF JUNAGADH, IN 1915AD *(TOP)* AND PRESENT-DAY *(BOTTOM)*

Junagadh

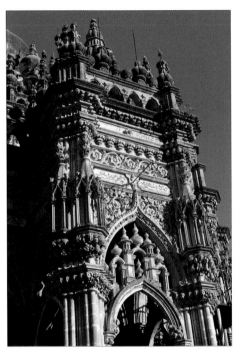

DETAIL OF THE INTRICATE FACADE OF THE 18TH CENTURY AD ROYAL MAQBARA

mid-16th century AD, and who took on the last name Babi after a member of the family. In the 1740s AD, Sher Khan Babi, foreseeing the ruins of the Mughal empire, began the process of carving out an independent kingdom for his family. He is known in history as Bahadur Khanji, and his descendants became the Babi dynasty Nawabs of Junagadh: Mahabat Khanji (1758-74AD), Hamed Khanji (1774-1811AD), Bahadur Khanji the second (1811-40AD), Hamed Khanji the second (1840-51AD), Mahabat Khanji the second (1851-82AD), Bahadur Khanji the third (1882-92AD), Rasul Khanji (1892-1911AD) and Mahabat Khanji the third

(1911-48AD).

Nawabi power was at its zenith in the 18th and 19th centuries AD. It was a force to reckon with, taking Zortalbi from a neighbouring princely state. Under Nawab Mahabat Khanji and Nawab Hamed Khanji, the Hindu diwan, Amar Sinhji, developed a powerful army, reportedly defeating even the Gaekwads of Baroda. But, instead of being proud of Amar Sinhji's achievements and encouraging him further to enrich his state, the nawabs, deciding that he had become too powerful for their good, had him killed in 1784AD.

Present-day Junagadh owes its picturesque cityscapes and pretty buildings to the rule of Nawab Mahabat Khanji the second, and his excellent diwan, Baha-ud-din, who was to be to his ruler in politics and management what Amar Sinhji had been to Nawab Mahabat Khanji in battle and defence. With the assistance of the British empire in India, the nawab and his diwan went to work on commissioning schools, colleges, markets, hospitals, courts and other buildings in the Venetian-Gothic style, and occasionally in oriental vein, epitomising the Victorian-Edwardian period in India.

The last of the nine nawabs, HH Nawab Sir Mahabat Khan GCSI, KCSI, was a great lover of nature, wildlife and domestic animals. He was the person responsible for the vigorous protection of the Gir forests, today the only important tract of forest land in the Saurashtra region and the last abode of

the Asiatic lion. He patronised Kathiawadi horses: the Kathi stud farm, still at Junagadh, owes its origin to the nawab. He imported many breeds of dog hitherto unknown to India, and is said to have taken an interest in improving the stock and milk yield of the Gir cattle. The nawab kept over 1,000 dogs, kennelled in considerable comfort, complete with servants, telephones, air conditioning and special foods. His favourite bitch, Roshanara, was raised in particular luxury and comfort. Her wedding to Bobby, a golden retriever belonging to the Nawab of Moangrol, was a grand affair, befitting a royal princess. A three days, state holiday was declared, and the citizens were entertained with sumptuous food, music, dancing girls and fireworks. The bridegroom's party was received by the nawab accompanied by 250 male dogs gorgeously attired in silks and jewellery. Red carpet treatment was given to Bobby, and an elephant procession with silver and

RANG MAHAL PALACE, JUNAGADH IN 1915AD

SUNSET OVER THE 19TH CENTURY AD ROYAL MAQBARA

government to take over and convert into monuments, public buildings and a museum.

Today, his nephews and nieces in Junagadh have come down to the mundane realities of the 20th century AD. Some of them are police officers, lawyers, businessmen, clerks, accountants, housewives and film actors. Note that Parveen Babi, a glamourous Hindu film star of the 1970s AD and early-1980s AD, is from this historic family!

The Uparkot fort crowns a hill on the outskirts of the city. The fort encompasses an area of around four square kilometres, with battlement walls some seventy feet high in places and moats inside believed by local people to be over three hundred feet deep, with a magnificent gateway leading into the fort. Practically the only standing structure in the fort is the Ranak Devi palace of the Chudasama Rajputs, with some intricate carved balconies still visible, which the sultan tried to convert into a mosque; but the subterranean enterprise here is no less impressive, with a network of Buddhist caves, which archaeologists believe date to the 2nd century AD, during the time of the Mauryan empire – and there are more Buddhist monastic caves in the surrounding hills. Then there is the 11th century AD Adi Chadi vav, a huge well with steps going down over one hundred feet to the water level, with some delightful folklore about the two slave girls after whom it is named; the 1070AD Navghan Khuva, a well said to be 340 feet deep with a 120 feet passage

gold howdahs took the bridegroom to the darbarhall for the marriage ceremony, which was conducted by priests, the bride wearing a beautiful pearl necklace and nothing else. The groom wore gold bracelets and a beautifully embroidered silk waistcoat. Once the marriage was consummated, Bobby was thrown into the kennels with the other dogs, whilst Roshanara continued to receive special consideration throughout her life. It is said that when he had to

allow the viceroys to shoot a lion in the Gir forests, his eyes filled with tears. As an administrator and as a man, he was respected by the masses. But when in 1947AD – it is said at the persuasion of his diwan, Bhutto, the ancestor of the famous Zulficar – he decided to join hands with Pakistan, he was denounced, outlawed, eventually outvoted and finally left with his harems, dogs and family for Pakistan. His palaces were left heirless for the

Junagadh

UPARKOT FORT RISING UP FROM THE HILLS ON THE OUTSKIRTS OF THE CITY OF JUNAGADH

UPARKOT FORT IN 1915AD

19TH CENTURY AD CITY PALACE OF JUNAGADH WHERE THE DARBARHALL IS LOCATED

spiralling down towards steps which descend right to the water level; and the British period Willingdon dam, a huge reservoir at the edge of the fort. There are also two cannon – the Nilam cannon, with the date of casting in Egypt (1531AD) inscribed in bronze, and the smaller Ottoman gun – which were brought here from Diu, after the port was lost to the Portuguese in 1536AD.

The city palace of the nawabs, built in the 1870s AD, is a short walk from the Uparkot fort gateway, and has now been converted into the darbarhall museum. The historic darbarhall offers a splendid insight into the rule of the Nawab of Junagadh, with magnificent European chandeliers and silk carpets setting off rows of silver-plated chairs, for the use of his heirs and advisers, leading to the throne of the nawab. The rooms and corridors of the palace

exhibit other reminders of the period. There is a room dedicated to the elephant howdahs and hand-held palanquins, adorned with mermaids and tigers beside velvet upholstered seats. Another room contains weaponry of the 19th century AD, including swords, daggers, turtle shell shields, medieval armour, guns and rifles; and yet a third is a gallery of portraits, paintings and old photographs. But the grandest reminders of the Babi dynasty's rule in Junagadh are the two royal maqbaras.

The 18th century AD maqbara buildings include some impressive domes, where columns meet intricate arches and horizontal cornices, and present a pleasant medieval flavour. The more recent 19th century AD maqbara are even more dazzling. One mausoleum evokes visions of St Petersburg. Another, even more splendid, holds the diwan Baha-ud-din,

and bears an almost fairground, Disney-like flamboyance, with spiralling staircases, silver doors, intricate facades and spired minarets.

Other palaces in Junagadh are now converted for use as public buildings: you can see the Rang mahal with its exquisite canvas ceilings, where it is said locally that the nawab kept his harem and pedigree dogs. The Sardarbagh garden palace is now a public park and houses government quarters and offices including the forest department. This palace has beautiful minarets and fountains, with noteworthy interior stucco carvings. Another palatial nawabi mansion, the Manoranjan circuit house, is a government guesthouse. You can see many other grand buildings in the city: the Reay Gate, a double storey crescent archway with a clock tower; the naya bazaar; and, perhaps best of all, the Baha-ud-din

Junagadh

College, with fabulous domes and exterior embellishments, and a majestic 160 square feet assembly hall with beautiful wooden bracketed galleries inside.

Outside the city of Junagadh, too, the nawabs had many palaces and country mansions. The nawab's lodge at Gir, in typical British colonial bungalow style with sloping roofs and cottage rooms, is now a forest guesthouse run by the government. The beach palace at Chorwad, a splendid palatial mansion facing the Arabian sea, with thick walls and Gothic arches, now belongs to the Tourism Corporation of Gujarat Ltd. The palace has old brass four-poster beds and a sea water swimming pool, for the beaches at Chorwad are too turbulent for swimming. Another sea-facing palace

of the Babi dynasty is at Veraval, now converted into a school.

The example of Junagadh is typical of the relationship which the princely states had with the political agent attached to Kathiawad, whether it was Sir J B Peile or Mr E H Percival, or, in earlier times, Colonel Hall Walker. The diwan was the link between the two, whether it was a matter of resolution of dispute, the granting of favours, or indeed of any other matter.

It is interesting to note that, in the year of his accession, Nawab Bahadur Khanji the third, appointed as his diwan a Hindu, Haridas Viharidas Desai, who had previously been diwan of Idar state, and still earlier of Wankaner and Wadhwan states during the minorities of their rulers.

One of the greatest works which the diwan oversaw was the construction of a railway joining the capital town, Junagadh, with Verawal, the principal port, so greatly expanding the railway system. He was held in such high esteem, even by the new nawab, Rasul Khanji, and the then British government that, while on a one-year sabbatical from Junagadh, he was appointed by Queen Victoria to be a member of the Royal Opium Commission, whose report was presented to Parliament in 1895AD. The only other Indian on the twelve-member commission was the Maharajah of Kapurthala. Upon Haridas Viharidas Desai's retirement, his brother, Sardar Rao Bahudar Bechardas Viharidas Desai, was appointed diwan.

RANG MAHAL PALACE AT JUNAGADH, PRESENT-DAY

ROYAL WEDDING, JUNAGADH 1915AD

The Princely State of Kutch

**17 GUN
SALUTE STATE**

**FROM A SURROUNDING HILL – BHUJIA FORT,
GUARDING THE CITY OF BHUJ**

Surrounded on one side by the Arabian sea, and the desert wilderness of Sindh, Rajasthan and the Rann of Kutch on the others, Kutch lies in splendid isolation, practically becoming an island during the monsoons when the Rann is inundated with rain, sea and river water. Yet the kingdom of Kutch remains one of the most respected in India, prosperous from trade with the cross-desert merchant caravans that connected north west Asia with the more fertile areas of Gujarat and southern India, and the seatrade vessels that ran from Africa, Arabia and the Persian Gulf to Calcutta on the eastern India coastline, docking en route at ports along the Gulf of Kutch.

The kingdom was founded by the Jadeja Rajputs, who claimed descent from Lord Krishna, who, like Christ, assumed the human form of God, and came down to earth to preach goodness and overcome evil. To India he gave the Bhagwat Gita, which is as sacred to Hinduism as the Bible is to Christianity, and the Koran to Islam. It is believed that 5,300 years ago, the sons of Lord Krishna were cursed by a meditating sage, whom they had disturbed, as a result of which their capital, Dwarka, was submerged by the sea. Aniruddha, one of the sons, escaped to Sindh and founded a kingdom there. Following a series of conflicts with the Arabs, some of the Rajput clans began to return to Dwarka, and took over the kingdom of Kutch, with the blessing of the sultans of Gujarat who ruled the whole area in the 1540s AD. After ruling for some time from Anjar, Maharao Khengarji, the first Jadeja Rajput ruler of Kutch, moved his capital to Bhuj, said to have been an outpost of the 2500-1500BC Indus valley civilisation, a stopover point for Alexander the Great when he invaded India, and the location of the classical Tej and Sulaimannagar cities described by early Muslim writers. The township was ideally

**THE 19TH CENTURY AD PRAGMAHAL PALACE
IN BHUJ**

located in the hinterland, between the sea port, the Banni grasslands and the Rann through which caravans arrived, and strategically protected by hills and the 160 metre high Bhujia hill fort, said to have been erected by the Naga chieftains before the

Kutch

arrival of the Rajputs. The town was further fortified with serpentine walls, thirty-five feet high and four feet thick, and given protection by fifty-one guns in the 1700s AD by Maharao Godji and his successor, Maharao Desalji.

Under the Rajputs, the ports of Kutch became important trading outposts. Ships carried grain, cotton, salt, textiles, spices, pottery and other products from India, and brought back rhino hide for armour, ivory and cloves from Zanzibar, and other goods from the Arabian-Persian ports. By the time the British had settled in India, around 800 ships operated out of Kutch, and the Kutchi merchants, most of them Bohra Muslims, had offices in almost every port of Arabia, Persia and Africa. Even the Mughals held the maharaos of Kutch in high esteem, as it was one of the very few kingdoms which had a navy strong enough to combat the Portuguese and other Europeans, which had taken over the important ports of Goa, Daman, Diu and Cochin – and which might provide a solution to the European competition that was robbing the Mughal empire of its income from seatrade. The maharaos were among the few rulers with the authority to mint their own coins, and were given important titles by Jehangir, the Mughal emperor.

The best of the palaces in Bhuj was the Aina mahal (literally translated, the palace of mirrors), erected in the 18th century AD by Maharao Lakhpat Sinh. A flamboyant ruler and patron of the arts,

Maharao Lakhpat Sinh commissioned the building of the palace to Ram Singh, who had been shipwrecked on an island in Europe, where he mastered the arts of glass blowing, tile making, stone carving, construction, enamelling, clock making and founding. Disappointed by a lack of patronage from the princes of Saurashtra, Ram Singh came to his native Kutch, and embellished the merchant mansions of Mandvi with his art. Maharao Lakhpat Sinh was impressed by Ram Singh's talents, and together the artisan and the patron of the arts constructed one of the most outstandingly beautiful palaces in the world. The king sent Ram Singh twice to Europe to learn more about Dutch and Venetian-Austrian techniques, and factories were set up in Kutch for glass, tiles and metalwork.

The Aina mahal palace is entered by a narrow, turning staircase, finishing in two intricate and perforated stonework screens, depicting entwining trees. The darbarhall, elegantly proportioned, is furnished in French style gilt wooden furniture, rather in the Louis XIV manner, and opposite it are a silver throne and a solid silver door. The wood pillared and intricately ceilinged galleries are now a museum of royal insignia, elephant-back howdah carriages, gilded copper objects, flags, palanquins, wooden chairs inlaid with glass of different colours, a scroll depicting scenes of the Nag pachami festival celebrations, and perfume spray; then there are embroidered caparisons for elephants, camels and

PRAGMAHAL PALACE SEEN FROM LAKE HAMIRSAR

UMBRELLA-LIKE DOME ON THE TERRACE OF THE VIJAY VILAS PALACE

Kutch

VIEW TOWARDS THE FROM THE COLONNADED TERRACE AT THE VIJAY VILAS PALACE

INTRICATE CARVINGS ON THE ZANANA OF THE VIJAY VILAS PALACE

INTRICATELY CARVED CHATTRIES OF VARIOUS GENERATIONS OF THE JADEJA RAJPUT RULERS OF KUTCH

horses, portraits, handfans – including some decorated with mica or made from silk – nutcrackers and various objects in agate, sandstone of Jaisalmer and Kutch, granite and wood. The velvet tent and other textiles depict patterns typical of the old silk trade route.

Beyond the darbarhall is the chamber of scribes, where writers and poets composed, singers and bards gave voice, and artists portrayed the lifestyles and glories of the rulers of Kutch. The hall now houses a collection of textiles including exquisite embroideries, silk fans and royal costumes. Its highlight, however, must be one of the most beautiful textiles of Indian origin in the world – a richly embroidered Ghagra skirt, embroidered with silk and covered with floral patterns. As many as seventeen colours can be detected in the skirt.

The prayer room has a fabulous image of the sun god on his seven-horse drawn carriage, kept alive by ceremonial objects like oil wick lamps, and a silver tray for offerings. Nevertheless, the pièce de résistance of the palace is the hall of mirrors, after which it is named. The walls of this hall are made from marble, covered with exquisite mosaics of multi-coloured glass in different patterns and

THE GATEWAY OF THE HATISTHAN WHERE THE MAHARAO HOUSED HIS ELEPHANTS

VIJAY VILAS PALACE OF THE MAHARAO OF KUTCH, ON THE MANDVI SEA COAST

PALIAS OR FUNERAL STONES AT DHANETI, NEAR BHUJ

mirrors in gilt frames, supplemented by an eclectic mix of wall decorations – you can see sketches by Hogarth, landscapes in local styles, etchings of buildings in England, Chinese glass paintings, drawings, cartoons, embroideries and Chinese tiles. From the ceiling and walls hang chandeliers, candelabra, Venetian glass lamps, brass lamps, ceiling lanterns called handis and an enormous hand operated fan embroidered with a peacock motif. In the centre is a pleasure pool, floored with Chinese tiles, and fed by an intricate system of fountains and pumps that could raise water from the ground without the need for electric power. Here, you can just imagine the pleasure-loving king watching dancing girls while he listened to bardic poetry.

The Hira mahal palace houses the private apartments, floored in blue and white tiles and embroidered carpets, enclosed by intricately carved pillars and walls covered with silk embroidered panels and mirror inlays. The rooms contain a strange mix of objects – paintings, clocks, globes, mechanical toys, daggers, weapons, floral glass, Venetian chandeliers and a bed and cupboard polished in gold. The whole palace is now open as a museum, and has a picture gallery of historic sepia toned photographs, portraits and paintings, most of them depicting life in the court and palaces of Kutch, including a likeness of Catherine the Great

Kutch

GALLERIES OF THE PRAGMAHAL PALACE, FLOORED IN MARBLE, AND ENCLOSED BY EUROPEAN COLUMNED ARCHES

THE DARBARHALL OF THE PRAGMAHAL PALACE, WITH RICHLY ORNAMENTED SURFACES, EUROPEAN STATUES, SHAKESPEAREAN CHARACTERS ON THE CEILINGS AND GALLERIES FACING THE HALL

and a painting of Maharao Lakhpat Sinh in the darbarhall, folk drawings, landscapes and contemporary objects of Kutch.

A beautiful marriage mandap, a set of thrones and tents made especially for the wedding of Maharao Khegarji the third, who married in 1884AD, is another highpoint of the palace. There is also a small card shop selling postcards, books and publications about Kutch, and souvenirs.

In front of the Aina mahal palace, where the public once petitioned its rulers, sits the Pragmahal palace, commissioned in the 1860s AD by Maharao Pragmalji, one of the best rulers of Kutch, and built by the English architect Colonel Wilkinson in an Italian Baroque style, and carved with balconies and stone jali work by Kutchi artisans. The palace inside is a blend of Victorian-Edwardian and Art Deco styles, having imposing staircases, arches, hunting trophies, stuffed animals, old photographs and beautiful European figures. The 25 x 12 metre darbarhall, with its twelve metre high ceiling, ornate verandahs, gilding, carving, ceiling paintings,

depicting scenes from Shakespearean plays, and stuffed animals is now a museum in part, and the outhouses and stables are now government offices.

Not satisfied with the Aina mahal palace in Bhuj, Maharao Lakhpat Sinh commissioned another fabulous palace in Mandvi, which, being an important port, had become a second capital of Kutch. As we have suggested earlier in this chapter, the Mughals would have given considerable importance to this port, representing as it did a possible solution to the European trade competition facing them in the east: Mandvi harboured one of the few navies that might repel the Portuguese invaders who had taken most of the important ports of western India already, and at the same time offered free access to Muslim pilgrims embarking for Mecca. In return, the Mughals gave almost complete autonomy to the Jadeja Rajput rulers of Kutch, including, as we have said earlier, the right to mint

SHARAD BAGH PALACE

their own coins, which were very popular locally.

The palace at Mandvi has intricate stone carvings, and a hall of mirrors similar to that in the Aina mahal palace. It is now a school for girls, rather in contrast to its original use as a place for the king to watch dancing girls.

The two palaces are said to have made a hole in the Kutchi treasury, and revolt ensued in the land of Kutch! There was pressure from potential invaders, who saw the weakness in Kutch, to the extent that the rulers left Mandvi for Bhuj, their strongest defended township. Mandvi became their summer home, where they retreated for the cool breezes that wafted across the sea into their pavilions.

In more optimistic times, the early-20th century AD saw the construction of the Vijay vilas palace, a strange medley of Mughal, Rajput and European styles: the sloping roofs of the British colonial style contrast with umbrella-like domes, rather like those seen in Rajasthan's Bikaner, and towers in the Muslim style; while Art Noveau windows juxtapose turrets and carved balconies that are strictly oriental.

Kutch

INTRICATE CARVINGS ON THE ARCHES OF THE ZANANA IN THE VIJAY VILAS PALACE

A SECTION OF THE CITY PALACE OF BHUJ WHICH IS NOW A SCHOOL

The magnificent palace has splendid views of the sea and of one of the most beautiful beaches in India, and inside you find spiralling staircases and galleries lined with stuffed animals and birds, old photographs and works of art.

Another of the turn-of-the-century AD work is the Sharad Bagh botanical gardens, enclosing a royal mansion which is now a museum of objects associated with the 20th century AD maharaos of Kutch, including the trophies won by the late Maharao Madan Sinhji in tennis and other sports.

But perhaps the greatest buildings relating to the royal families of Kutch are not the palaces and forts, but the chattries, the mausolea of the Hindu kings. The memorial tombs are made from red sandstone and are intricately carved. The best is the one of Maharao Lakhpat Sinh, dating from the 1770s AD, with a splendidly carved roof supported by pillars and with beautiful carved statues of gods and the king inside – flamboyant in death as in life! Around the memorial are scattered tablets of beautifully carved stone, depicting people who committed suicide on his pyre.

Other royal initiatives were the Ramkund stepped well, made from intricate carved red sandstone, and the Hatisthan, where elephants were housed.

The maharaos of Kutch, often prone to revolt from their subjects, had a number of forts and castles in the surrounding barren hills and arid plains – it has been said that there are one hundred forts in Kutch – and those in the villages of Gadsisa, Roha and Virani are noted for their intricate stone carvings, while the castle at Tera village is known for its frieze of frescos depicting the Hindu epic poem the Ramlila.

The Princely State of Limbdi

**9 GUN
SALUTE STATE**

The rulers of Limbdi belonged to the Jhala Rajput clan which came to Patdi from Sindh. They were among the first of the four salute state and five non-salute state rulers of the Jhala Rajput clan to separate from the elder clan at Halwad, which is now in Dhrangadhra. Mangoji, the second son of Harpaldeo Sinh, who ruled from Patdi, founded the state of Limbdi.

One of the most popular rulers of Limbdi was Thakore Saheb Rana Sir Jaswant Sinhji, who ruled in the late-19th and early-20th centuries AD. During his schooling at Rajkumar College, Jaswant Sinhji was described as one of the most promising princes in Saurashtra, and won prizes for sport, progress and conduct. He was one of the first rulers of Saurashtra to venture to Europe, where he met the British royal family, the Empress of Germany, the Duke of Connaught, the Earls of Northbrooke and Dufferin, the Marquises of Lansdowne and Ripon, and Lord and Lady Salisbury. He returned bearing a silver medal of recognition from HRH The Prince of Wales.

Back in India, he associated with the judiciary, and learned about jurisdiction, and it was on the recommendation of the judiciary that he was given the throne while still a minor. His reforms to the judicial structure and municipal and public works at Limbdi, which served to improve the lot of agricultural communities through a committee of twenty-four people set up to supervise municipal affairs under his guidance, and irrigation systems in particular, won him praise from Lord Reay and Sir James Ferguson. He represented his region in the Legislative Council, and introduced new reforms to the Council, even going against his European colleagues. The English school at Limbdi received

ENTRANCE TO THE DIGBHUVAN

Limbdi

ENTRANCE TO THE 19TH CENTURY AD CITY PALACE OF LIMBDI

PART OF THE OLD CITY PALACE, WHICH IS NOW THE CENTRAL MARKETPLACE

his patronage, and he introduced important scholarships. Despite his admiration for western countries, and his interest in promoting English education, he remained close to his Indian roots, and a strong believer in Lord Shiva and in

EXTENSIVE GROUNDS OF THE DIGBHUVAN

Vedic philosophy.

The old palace of Limbdi is in the European style with a Venetian-Gothic facade and century-old clock tower. Leading to the palace are buildings in the Regency style, which must have formed part of the palace at one time, but are now the central marketplace. The palace is now given over to a religious trust.

The family occupies the Digbhuvan, a European guesthouse with impressive Classical pillars and wide porticos. A highlight of the palace is an imposing staircase, with intricate stained glass windows on the landing. The Indian hunting theme on the glass suggests that it must have been custom-made for a thakore saheb of Limbdi. The present owner,

Thakore Saheb Chatrashailya Sinh, is a keen angler and lover of motor cars, and a successful businessman who owns a motel in Morvi and has numerous other business interests which he conducts from offices within the palace.

THAKORE SAHEB CHATRASHAILYA SINH OF LIMBDI

The Princely State of Morvi

11 GUN SALUTE STATE

The picturesque town of Morvi, located at the tip of the Kathiawadi peninsula where it begins to give way to Kutch, was actually part of the kingdom of Kutch, and ruled by the Jadeja Rajputs from the 16th century AD. Numerous are the intriguing stories about how Morvi became an independent state. One of them tells us that the ruler of Kutch gifted the kingdom of Morvi to his son, Rangji or Ravaji, an act that immediately caused a revolt among his other sons, who recognised the strategic importance of Morvi in controlling trade between Kutch and other parts of Gujarat. One of the brothers, Pragmalji, had Rangji assassinated and took back the kingdom, but in the skirmishes that followed, Rangji's son, Kavoji, defeated his uncle and captured Morvi. However, over the next few generations, Morvi remained in a constant state of flux, and internal strife and skirmishes were frequent.

Aloiji succeeded Thakore Saheb Kavoji in 1729AD, and developed the port of Vavania on the eastern edge of the Gulf of Kutch. Following his death at the hand of an assassin, he was succeeded by Thakore Saheb Ravaji the second, who ruled from 1772-85AD, and who fought many battles and extended the kingdom. It was during his rule that the fort wall around the town was built. Thakore Saheb Hamirji, his successor, was involved in battles with the Jhalas of Wadhwan, and during the rule of his son Thakore Saheb Jiaji, there were attacks from Meru Khwas, from the maharaos of Kutch, who wanted to take over Vavania port, and from the

BUILT IN 1882AD, THE DARBARGADH OF MORVI RISES UP FROM THE BANKS OF THE RIVER MACHCHU

INSIDE THE ENTRANCE TO THE DARBARGADH OF MORVI

Miana tribe, who were angered by his invasion of Maliya. Even after the Walker Settlement, which brought about peace between the rulers of Saurashtra, the princes of Morvi continued to be given special protection. It was left to HH Maharajah Waghji, who came to the throne in 1879AD, to prove that Saurashtra might be ruled ably, and this he did immediately, going to work to develop Morvi into a first class princely state and to equip it with a fine palace.

The darbargadh of Morvi, built in 1882AD, is an eclectic mixture of Indian and Venetian-Gothic styles, rising up on the banks of the river Machchu. Seen from the river, it looks like a palatial mansion of Venice, with shady logias, Venetian-Gothic arches and European roofs. To the front elevation and in the centre courtyard, however, Classical pillars and Gothic arches consort with Rajput jarokhas and

Islamic domes – here a pointed Gothic arch window is framed by curved Rajput arches, and there an Italianesque balustrade or Grecian urn gives way to a Mughal pavilion. The interiors are now being restored.

Across the river from the darbargadh is the Nazzar bagh palace, which was once the garden palace of the eight wives' harem of HH Maharajah Waghji. The ruler found it tiresome to have to make his way through town in order to visit the palace, but solved the problem after visiting Italy and seeing an amusing little suspension bridge, which he went on to duplicate in Morvi. The bridge, now open to the public, was then used only by members of the royal family, and the household staff, who had to remove their footwear before walking across.

The maharajah's favourite wife was Manibai, and upon her death he went into mourning, giving up many worldly pleasures. For some time after her death he even prohibited the wearing of brightly coloured clothing in Morvi. In her memory, he went to work on a 220 room palace called Mani mandir, attached to a temple – which was intended to be open to the people – but which remained incomplete on his death in 1922AD. HH Maharajah Lakhadir Sinhji, who succeeded him, was his son by another marriage to a princess of Palitana, and thus his feelings for the late Manibai, perhaps understandably as his mother's rival for the maharajah's affections, were somewhat restrained.

He had the Mani mandir completed, but re-named it Wagh mandir, though, fittingly enough, the people of Morvi still call it Mani mandir. The palace, with its apparently myriad rooms on layer upon layer of floors, is an amazing piece of Rajput architecture: uncounted cupolas are supported by balustrades on the terrace, while intricately carved jarokha balconies protrude from the facade. The building looms every bit as impressively as the darbargadh, a short distance from the banks of the same river.

But HH Maharajah Waghji was known not only for his palace building. He was also a great administrator. During his rule, internal security measures were strictly imposed, and bandits driven from the land. Excellent roads and railways were introduced, and a tramway built to connect Morvi to Wadhwan. The port of Vavania, the pride of his ancestors, was developed further to take small ocean-going vessels, and a new port at Naulakha was developed.

Commerce and industry prospered, and the local production of textiles and salt found its way overseas. Unlike his contemporary, HH Maharajah Bhagwat Sinhji of Gondal, who was a thoroughly democratic and benevolent ruler, HH Maharajah Waghji was very feudal in his outlook, indeed his policies sometimes bordered on the tyrannical. Newspapers were banned, and one could not speak one's mind openly. The maharajah did not allow moneylenders to operate in his kingdom, preferring

MAHARANI VIJAYKUVERBA WITH HER FOUR DAUGHTERS, RAUKHSMANI, DRAUPATI, UMA AND PURNA

to give loans from the state treasury to farmers and industry. Unlike HH Maharajah Bhagwat Sinhji, he was a flamboyant man, fond of his luxuries and comforts, and he shared this trait with his neighbouring ruler, HH Maharajah Amar Sinhji of Wankaner. He was one of the first of several princes of Saurashtra to own his own aircraft, in addition to a fleet of cars, horse drawn carriages and railway saloon carriages. During the Second World War, the

family donated its Spitfire aeroplane to the Allies' war effort.

During HH Maharajah Waghji's rule and that of his son, HH Maharajah Lakdhir Sinhji, Morvi saw the addition of many interesting architectural showpieces: among them the clock tower, and the crowned town gate, supposed to be a replica of the Eiffel Tower in Paris. One of the several bridges in the town had its statues of the maharajah's favourite horses, Dollar and Star, replaced by a pair of bulls after he was inspired by bull fights in Spain during a visit to Europe. But the local population could not identify with the bulls, so dissimilar were they to the ones found in Gujarat, and thought rather that they were buffaloes. And the bridge today is called Pada Pool – the bridge of the buffaloes!

HH Maharajah Lakdhir Sinhji was succeeded by his son, HH Maharajah Mahendra Sinhji. An all round sportsman, and in particular a keen equestrian and owner of numerous race horses in England and India, it was he who signed the Act of Accession in 1947AD.

His widow, Maharani Vijaykuverba, spends most of her time in her beloved Morvi. She has four daughters, Raukhsmani, Draupati, Uma and Purna, and two grandchildren, Leah and Vishal. Passionately patriotic and a popular figure in Morvi, the maharani is actively involved in numerous charitable activities through the Mayur Foundation, named after her late and only son, Mayur, and through the Lakdhir Sinhji Foundation, named after her late husband's father. The maharani has also set up her own personal foundation for the treatment of cancer, tuberculosis, heart disease and cataract patients, and to finance a pharmacy which dispenses free medicines. A piece of paper may have stripped the ruling families of their powers and titles, but the Rajput tradition of looking after the weak and needy of society is not so easily lost.

FRONT GATEWAY TO THE DARBARGADH OF MORVI

INTERIOR VIEW OF THE ENTRANCE TO THE DARBARGADH

The Princely State of Palanpur

13 GUN SALUTE STATE

NAWAB IQBAL MUHAMMAD KHAN GREETING KING GEORGE VI

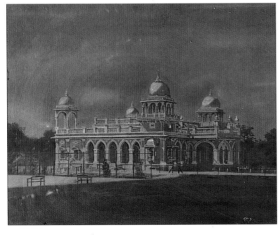

PAINTING DEPICTING THE SHAHIBAGH, BEFORE INDEPENDENCE

Tales abound of how the humble Pathans from Lohan in Afghanistan, who came to Bihar seeking employment, became the rulers of Jalore and established a strong Lohani dynasty that ultimately became the nawabi family of Palanpur. The most plausible concerns that of one Malek Khuram Khan, who moved from Bihar to Marwar in Rajasthan, and got a job in the court of Vishaldev Sinh, the ruler of Mandore, the capital of Marwar, in the 1390s AD. He was eventually appointed to handle the affairs of Jalore, the south western section of Marwar, a kingdom comparable in size to some of the smaller European nations. The death of Vishaldev Sinh brought chaos to Marwar. Courtiers against Khuram Khan had poisoned the queen, and in the skirmishes and confusion that followed, Khuram Khan took control of Jalore and declared himself ruler of Jalore principality.

A shrewd ruler, Khuram Khan wrote a letter to the Muslim governor of Gujarat, to inform him that Sultan All-a-ud-din Khilji had captured the fort of Jalore, but lost it again to the Rajputs of Marwar. In taking Jalore, he informed the governor, he had brought that city under the Islamic flag. The letter

pleased the sultan, who replied, promising assistance in administration and battle, something that gave Khuram Khan a powerful position. As luck would have it, however, Khuram Khan was killed in a duel for supremacy with neighbouring ruler, Trimmanna Solanki. His son, Malek Yusuf Khan, avenged his father's death by killing Trimmanna, and seized the throne of Jalore.

Holding on to a principality surrounded by such major powers as Mewar, Marwar and Sirohi, was not easy. Battles were frequent, and fighting between relatives and usurping of the throne not uncommon. Numerous poems have been written about wars waged between the Lohani rulers of Jalore and the Rajputs, including some involving rival potential heirs to the Jalore throne taking assistance from different powers – the one from the Maharana of Mewar, the other from the Sultan of Gujarat, for instance. Equally, the generosity of the Lohanis, who gave villages, land and gifts to poets and priests, both Hindu and Muslim, is also well documented by the bards.

Meanwhile, the Rathore Rajputs had taken Marwar from the descendants of Vishaldev Sinh and

Palanpur

HH Nawab Saheb Sher Khan Babi

Shahibagh, present-day

HH Nawab Saheb Zorawar Khan sporting sword gifted by an Mughal emperor

HH Nawab Saheb Sir Taley Muhammad Khan of Palanpur *(right)* **with the rulers of Kashmir** *(left)* **and Limbdi** *(standing)*

Remains of one of the old palaces of Palanpur

Maqbara of the rulers of Palanpur

HH Nawab Saheb Sher Khan Babi with his sons

BALARAM PALACE NOW RESTORED TO ITS FORMER GLORY

THE GARDENS OF BALARAM PALACE, LANDSCAPED TO THE ORIGINAL NAWABI DESIGN

moved the capital from Mandore to Jodhpur in 1449AD. Close ties were drawn between Jodhpur and the Mughal emperors of Delhi, and in the early-17th century AD, Emperor Jehangir issued a directive transferring the rule of Jalore to Marwar. The Lohanis of Jalore rose up in revolt, but were defeated, and Pahad Khan Lohani began to move down to the Aravali foothills of Gujarat, in search of a new capital.

The Lohanis had settled in the 12th century AD in the plains of north Gujarat, just short of the Aravali mountain range, where a stretch of prime grassland had provided grazing pastures for horses and cattle of the Solanki Rajput kings of Gujarat in the 11th century AD. Palanpur had grown into an important city under Palandeo Sinh, who had been appointed to rule this region after the Muslims conquered Gujarat in the 13th century AD, and finally had become a centre of learning and commerce when Emperor Akhbar came to the throne of Delhi. Diwan Firoz Khan Lohani was given gifts and recognition from the Mughal emperor for crushing revolts and bringing to heel the dreaded outlaw, Kanji Koli, in the 1630s AD and 1640s AD.

The golden age for Palanpur dawned when – after the death of HH Nawab Saheb Joravar Khan in 1877AD – HH Nawab Saheb Sher Khan Babi was placed on the throne by the British for rendering help during the 1857AD mutiny. HH Nawab Saheb Sher Khan Babi set about improving the quality of agriculture; he introduced schools for boys and girls, a hospital and other medical services, and a library; he improved rail and road links, and saw sixty-eight villages populated. Advances were made to farmers to improve yields and to dig wells. Primary education was free for all.

HH Nawab Saheb Sher Khan Babi was succeeded in 1917AD by HH Nawab Saheb Sir Taley Muhammad Khan, a man who, as crown prince, had already begun to make his mark, especially in diplomatic relations with the British, in forging friendships with important princely states, and in

Palanpur

establishing cordial relations with his subjects. While some recall his eccentricities – his walking sticks were carved so as to resemble the heads of different breeds of pedigree dogs – he is better remembered for establishing the King George V Club in 1913AD, in order to introduce important people at the court of Palanpur to British customs and sports, so that they would not be conspicuous during meetings with viceroys or the British political agents at banquets or at official functions.

During his rule, state revenue increased and cultivation of potatoes was undertaken along the river Banas. Plans were laid to introduce a judiciary and a legislature, but they were thwarted first by the events of 1939-45AD, and finally in 1947-48AD by Independence. So close were relations between HH Nawab Saheb Sir Taley Muhammad Khan and the British that, as the stroke of midnight of 14th August 1947AD approached, Lord Mountbatten decided to favour his good friend by signing a document recognising his Australian wife as Begum Jahanara, the Queen of Palanpur. It was a rare thing indeed for foreign wives to be accepted as queens by the British government! "It is best to be practical in today's world," HH Nawab Saheb Sir Taley Muhammad Khan's son, Nawab Iqbal Muhammad

Khan Lohani, told me. For him, that meant relinquishing his vast and unmanageable palaces of Palanpur for his apartment in Bombay; for his sons, it meant setting up their own businesses, including Contemporary Arts and Crafts, a well known store in Bombay.

The Zorawar palace in Palanpur was probably founded by HH Nawab Saheb Zorawar Khan in the 1850s AD, and has obviously been extended by

KIRTI MANDIR, A MONUMENT TO THE ROYAL FAMILY OF PALANPUR

PAINTING OF THE ORIGINAL ZOROWAR PALACE

VIEW FROM BALARAM PALACE TO THE WOODED HILLS THAT ONCE PROVIDED THE FAMILY WITH GAME, NOW A WILDLIFE SANCTUARY

ENTRANCE LOBBY OF BALARAM PALACE

MAQBARA OF THE RULERS OF PALANPUR

HH NAWAB SAHEB SIR TALEY MUHAMMAD KHAN
(LEFT) WITH HH MAHARAJAH GANGA SINHJI OF
BIKANER (RIGHT)

successive rulers, HH Nawab Saheb Sher Khan Babi and HH Nawab Saheb Sir Taley Muhammad Khan. The palace spans a huge area and is a synthesis of different styles – tapering Bengali style umbrella domes, Indo-Saracenic domes, turrets, Rajput style jarokha balconies and fretwork jali screens. A highlight of the palace is the banqueting hall, now a district court, with beautiful ceiling frescos between intricate mouldings, giving a three-dimensional effect, gold and silver paintwork, ornate doors and a fabulous fireplace. A massive staircase, carved in sandalwood, leads up to chambers that are now used by the judge and the magistrates. Intricate marble statues stand in the forecourt of a part of the palace, now a police station.

The only section retained by the family is Shahibagh, an old guesthouse, now the residence, with the nawab's collection of antique furniture, crystal, paintings, hunting trophies and artefacts. Several older palaces of Palanpur are now in ruins.

Impressive to this day is the cluster of maqbaras built for the nawabs, with exquisite cusped arches, intricate jali screens and incredibly beautiful stone sculpture.

Fourteen kilometres from Palanpur, HH Nawab Saheb Sir Taley Muhammad Khan built the Balaram palace as a hunting lodge, holiday palace and riverside retreat, inspired it is said, by his Australian queen. This is where he entertained important guests like the Maharajah of Kashmir and British

CUSPED ARCHWAYS OF THE MAQBARA OF THE RULERS OF PALANPUR

ZOROWAR PALACE, NOW A COURT OF LAW

VIEWS FROM BALARAM PALACE TO THE GARDENS AND HILLS BEYOND

dignitaries. The palace is in a neo-Classical Baroque style, with arcades and Classical columns. It has now been taken over by a private entrepreneur, and opened as a resort. The huge gardens, their contours clearly defined, have been landscaped to blend exotic plants, bridges and ramps for easy access into the original Nawabi design. The entrance pathway is lit by lampposts resembling parabadis, the traditional bird feeding posts of Gujarat. The facade has been painted in a gracious creamy tone, and glass has been added to protect the interiors from dust. The interiors have been newly appointed, as the original furniture was stolen, with modern handcrafted pieces, and western style bathrooms, televisions, telephones and refrigerators have been added to the rooms for the modern traveller. A feature of the property is the swimming pool, fed by a natural rock spring, half-way up the bluff, on which the palace sits facing the river Balaram, with the overflow dripping into the river below. The new owners have created an artificial cascade from the rock spring to the pool to replace the previous trickle. An old wall has been extended to house a modern gymnasium. The cellars of the palace, with brick lined arches, once contained the finest of wines, but are now an indoor games centre for children. The forests that once provided the family and their guests with game are now a sanctuary for bear, panther and other wildlife.

The Princely State of Patdi

NON- SALUTE STATE

THE OLD FORT OF PATDI, ITS FORTIFIED WALLS STILL INTACT, SURROUNDS TYPICAL BRITISH COLONIAL STYLE BUILDINGS

The original Patels or Patidars came in the 17th century AD to Gujarat in small bands, probably small breakaway fighting groups of larger invading armies in the north of India. They either displaced the Brahim landlord caste from areas where they were entrenched, or just laid claim to large land areas and started cultivating. They utilised the local tribes as farm labour, and for clearing large tracts of natural forest and vegetation for agricultural use. Even collectively, they were too small and disorganised a fighting unit to be a threat, and only for the revenue they generated for their state were they tolerated by the Rajput and Muslim rulers of the area. Setting social norms in order to define their 'Patidar-hood', they established themselves as a hard working and enterprising community. They prospered, as many parts of Gujarat are blessed with rich and fertile soil: areas like Charotar, the central part of Kaira district, and the ancestral home of the author.

The requirement to use a surname, not a common practice in Gujarat, was introduced by the British, and the surname Patel, meaning landowner or farmer, was taken up by many other communities in Gujarat.

A small, non-salute state, Patdi would not normally feature in our book, but for the fact that the rulers were not Muslim, Rajput or Marathas, but Patels.

The Patels or Patidars claim descent from Rama, and are divided into Levas and Kadvas, names which originate from those of the two sons of Rama, Lav and Kush.

Patdi

THE OLD DARBARGADH FORT OF PATDI, BUILT PARTIALLY BY THE JHALAS, WHO LATER MOVED TO DHRANGADHRA

RAGHU VILAS PALACE, THE CURRENT RESIDENCE OF THE PATDI FAMILY

Large families over several generations – families with twelve children were not uncommon – and improved life expectancy resulted in descendants inheriting very small parcels of the land originally enclaved by their ancestors. This, together with natural disasters like drought, floods and plagues of locusts at the close of the 20th century AD, caused considerable distress to farmers and resulted in the Patidars branching out into other trades and professions. With easy access through Gujarat's ports, and trade links with the rest of the world, a large number of Patels emigrated, some as far afield as Fiji in the Pacific ocean. The majority, however, emigrated to East Africa and from there on to England and the United States. Patels can be found in virtually any large city telephone directory around the world. Accounts of their enterprise and industry abound.

The author's father, Shantilal Parbhoodas Patel, left his ancestral village of Dharmaj in 1945AD. As the youngest of four sons, he inherited very little land, not enough to support a family. He sailed to Beira in Mozambique, and sought his fortune in Northern Rhodesia (now Zambia) and then, finally, in California, USA.

Jhaverbhai Patel, born in 1829AD in Karamsad, the ancestral village of the author's mother, and of whom she was a distant relative, owned ten acres of land there. He had five sons and a daughter. Ten acres divided between five sons would not sustain five families. The fourth born son, Vallabhbhai, born in 1875AD, together with an elder brother, joined the legal profession. The two brothers practiced in the area and made a name for themselves. Encouraged by their success, they decided to go to England. There they qualified as barristers before returning to settle in Ahmedabad.

In 1913AD, Vallabhbhai entered politics. Vallabhbhai's sympathy for Indian nationalism had come from his father, who had gone off to fight the British, taking the side of a local war lord in the 1857AD mutiny. He had spent the winter nights of

Patdi

THE AUTHOR DR HANSDEV PATEL WITH DILIP SINHJI DESAI PATEL, BENEATH ANCESTRAL PORTRAITS

his boyhood listening to his father's old-soldier tales of the mutiny. As a young man he sought out Gandhi, and offered him his services. In 1922AD, Gandhi, anxious to see what civil disobedience might achieve, asked Vallabhbhai Patel to organize an experimental campaign in 137 villages in Bardoli. In the event, his organization was so comprehensive, so thorough, that the campaign succeeded beyond even Gandhi's hopes. From then on, Vallabhbhai Patel shared with Nehru the position just below Gandhi's in the independence movement. He went on to become deputy Prime Minister and Home Minister in independent India. He was known as the iron man of Indian politics and was called Sardar – meaning born to lead! He was responsible for the rulers of the princely states renouncing their temporal powers, abandoning their claim to autonomy and acceding to the Indian Union. This was an historic and noteworthy achievement, in that the absolute powers which the rulers for centuries had enjoyed over their land and their subjects, were relinquished by the stroke of a pen and without the loss of a single human life. This ultimate act of true patriotism on the part of the princely families has never really been given the credit it deserves.

Patdi itself had been the capital of the Jhala Rajputs from the 12th century AD to the 15th century AD, but a peaceful edict issued by the Sultan of Gujarat, Ahmed Shah, had transferred the rights over the villages around Patdi to the Muslim talukdars of Dasada and to some Patel jamindars, The Patel jamindars of Patdi found themselves having to give up their agricultural efforts, and were given the power of rule in return for their assistance to the British. The present owners of the old fort are descendants of the Patel jamindars.

The old fort of Patdi is splendidly located on the shores of a lake, which must have provided adequate protection to the old walls. The Jhala Rajputs still have their ancestral temples in the fort, and sponsored some of its reconstruction even after they moved capital first to Halwad, and then Dhrangadhra, and eventually divided into separate states like Wankaner and Wadhwan. The fort walls are still intact, but the buildings inside, many of which, judging by the European style architecture and trussed timber and rafter roofs, date to the British colonial period, are in a dilapidated condition. The trees around the fort are used as nesting grounds by a variety of birds, including colonies of painted storks. The main fort is still owned by the Patdi darbars, but some of the land within the walls has been purchased by the rulers of Dhrangadhra, to protect their ancestral temples.

The present official residence of the Patdi darbars is the Raghu vilas palace, built in Italian style with Classical columns, trussed roofs and Gothic arches. A huge wrought iron gate marks the entrance. The forecourt takes the form of a garden, with shady trees and benches. Intricate wood carvings can be seen around the palace. The family now lives in Ahmedabad, in an old pre-Independence bungalow called Patdi House.

The head of the family, Dilip Sinhji Desai Patel, is a keen collector of Indian antiques and recounted to me with pride that, for over two centuries, a Hindu Patel darbar had administered and ruled benignly over an area dominated by a large Muslim population. His state is close to the Pakistan border and the Little Rann of Kutch, and his knowledge of the local area is said to have played an important part during India's war with Pakistan in 1965AD. His sons have numerous business interests, including a magnesia plant and salt works in the Rann of Kutch, together with investments in textiles and cattle.

The Princely State of Porbandar

13 GUN SALUTE STATE

THE DARIA RAJMAHAL AT PORBANDAR BUILT IN 1900AD WITH A CLASSICAL FACADE BLENDS ARABIC, INDIAN AND RENAISSANCE STYLES

INNER COURTYARD SHOWING GALLERIES AT THE DARIA RAJMAHAL

Located on the shores of the Arabian sea, with creeks jutting into the city scenery, Porbandar was the capital of the Jethwa dynasty, which is believed to have come to the Kathiawadi peninsula from Kashmir around 2,000 years ago. The dynasty claimed descent from the Hindu wind god, Pawan, and so shares its lineage with Lord Hanuman, a Hindu god depicted as half-monkey and half-man. The Jethwas are certainly one of the oldest dynasties of Gujarat and Saurashtra, though the origin of their name is less certain. One possibility is that they descended from the Yetha clan of the Huns. It is also argued that they are perhaps descendants of Jyeshthamitra Shung, grandson of Pushyamitrs Shung, King of Magda, who ruled from 185BC to 149BC, and who had a son called Jetha. Jetha ventured to Gujarat to fight the Bactrian Greeks, who had established their sway over Kutch and Saurashtra. He probably did not return from the expedition, as the history book of the Shung Dynasty says nothing about Jetha after his invasion of Saurashtra. It is probable that Jetha died here, and his son, finding that Vasumitra would not let him enter Magda, stayed over and ruled over a part of the country. As was the custom, he would have dropped the surname Shung and adopted Jethwa, meaning 'sons of Jetha'.

Porbandar

DINING HALL AT THE HUZOOR PALACE

INTERIOR OF HUZOOR PALACE, WITH STUFFED GIR LION

There were 185 princes of the Jethwa dynasty, the last of whom was the ruler of the princely state of Porbandar, HH Maharana Natwarsinhji.

The Jethwas ruled from a town beside the river Machchu, probably present-day Morvi. The prosperous lands of Gujarat, located near the turbulent regions of Rajasthan and Sindh, attracted rulers, warriors, invaders and refugees, and the Jethwas always found themselves in a position of contrasting fortunes – now ruling a major part of Gujarat, now dethroned.

Porbandar is probably the city of Pauravelakul mentioned in the 10th century AD inscriptions at Ghumli and the Sundamapuri mentioned in the Hindu epic, Mahabharata, and Krishnalila, the story of Lord Krishna. Bardic poetry of Kathiawad is full of stories of Jethwa rulers like Halaman and Nagarjoon, stories of romantic warrior skills, valour and even spiritual powers.

On a stronger historic footing, inscriptions of the 9th to 11th centuries AD indicate that the Jethwas ruled the western corner of Kathiawad from Ghumli. Ghumli, the Jethwa capital mentioned in the inscriptions, is now a crumbling ruin, but even dilapidation cannot conceal some spectacular works of medieval architecture. The early-12th century AD

Vikia vav, which has splendidly decorated pavilions, is a stepped well, which, unlike the plain, cylindrical wells of Europe, had steps leading down to the water level, the passage walls string-coursed with carvings and sculpture.

A stepwell usually doubled as a subterranean palace for the ruler, with chambers cooled by the well water and underground location, and sometimes served as a resting place for merchant caravans seeking escape from the sun and a cooling drink. Nearby stands a Hindu temple, situated on a plinth, with pointed dome roofs called shikaras and a multi-pillared courtyard. The eroded surfaces still

Porbandar

HUZOOR PALACE, AT THE EDGE OF THE SEA

HH MAHARANA HERENDRA DE SILVA QC

show evidence of splendid carvings and sculpture.

The dynasty faced a number of problems, including invasion by the Jadeja Rajputs, who defeated them in battle in the late-16th and early-17th centuries AD. The Jethwas returned to power in the 1630s AD, when the Jam Saheb of Nawanagar (present-day Jamnagar) granted them Ranpur, which they made their capital. From there, they moved to Chaya which became their capital. They ruled from an impressive darbargadh, now in total disrepair, but with a fabulous carved jarokha balcony, bringing to the mind of the spectator the impressive scale of the Jethwa kingdom of that time. Porbandar was by then an important port: it had flourished from trade with the Arabian and African ports in medieval times, and more recently has become known for its exports via the ports of Bombay and Karachi. Persian inscriptions show that, in the late-17th century AD, Savji Parikh, with a team of other traders from Porbandar, approached the Mughal emperor Shah Jahan, and succeeded in negotiating a tax reduction from 6% to 5%. Savji Parikh was given a roll of

honour, called a tampatra, from Maharana Sartanji for this achievement. It was during this time, too, that Maharana Sartanji had walls built around Porbandar to protect the city from invaders, with five gates guarded by Arab warriors.

By the 18th century AD, the Jethwas had finally settled at Porbandar, and, in 1784AD, Maharana Sartanji built the darbargadh, in the wood and stone carved style typical of Gujarat. The remains of this palace can still be seen in the centre of Porbandar. An even greater architectural achievement, and set in a pleasant garden, was the Grishmabhuvan, a pleasure pavilion with impressive domes, exquisite pillars meeting in carved capitals and delicate arches. This pavilion, also called Sartanji choro (four sides) for its four parts representing the different seasons, was Maharana Sartanji's refuge from the crowds of Porbandar, where he retired to read and write poetry. You can imagine the sea breezes wafting into the pavilion on the third storey, with its cusped arches and stone columns so intricately carved they look just like wood, before later buildings all but obstructed the sea views from that vantage point.

In apparent self-contradiction, Maharana Sartanji, the poet and writer, was also known for his marksmanship! Locals believed that, even blindfolded, he could take accurate aim, guided only by the sound emanating from his target.

Porbandar occupied a unique position as a port city. It was strategically situated south of the ports of

Nawanagar and Kutch states, and north of Veraval in Junagadh state, and historically had traded with Arabian gulf and African countries. The creamy coloured stone of Porbandar had been a major export in days gone by, and was used in many of the Victorian period buildings of Bombay and Karachi. The skilled artisans of Porbandar were experts at making dhows by hand, and gave birth to an industry of building ocean-going vessels.

In 1807AD, the British brought peace to Saurashtra through the Walker Settlement. Peace reigned, and this was the time for the Jethwa rulers to start developing Porbandar. Rajmata Rupaliben, the queen mother, commissioned a freshwater reservoir in Porbandar in the 1850s AD. Separate schools for boys and girls were built in 1865AD, as were a post office, and buildings for other services. The old fort walls were pulled down to enlarge the city, and a town hall, railway station, lighthouse and the Jubilee Bridge were erected in the 1880s AD. Porbandar was also the birthplace of arguably the world's best loved Indian: the diwan bungalow

Porbandar

HH Maharana Bhav Sinhji

HH Maharana Natwarsinhji and his European wife, Maharani Anant Kunverba

where Mahatma Gandhi was born on 2nd October 1869AD is now the Kirti mandir, a memorial to the great man, with a museum of his effects. The Gandhi family were the hereditary diwans of Porbandar. Karamchand Gandhi, father of Mohandas Karamchand Gandhi, held the post in the 1860s AD, before moving the family to Rajkot, where Gandhiji spent his school days, later going to university at Bhavnagar, and then travelling to England and South Africa, where he was inspired to take up the causes of justice and truth.

At the turn of the 20th century AD, HH Maharana Bhav Sinhji came to the throne, and started a process of rapid reform. In 1900AD, he built the Daria rajmahal, Porbandar's sea-facing city palace, in a style that blends Arabic, Indian, Gothic and Renaissance architecture. The entrance is through a Gothic style archway, crowned by a tall tower that offers stunning views of the palace courtyards, to the beaches beyond the courtyard and to the sea. The centre of the palace is a courtyard with a garden, Italianesque fountains and galleries. Around the courtyard rises the palace, with numerous tiers of arches and heavily embellished facades rising up to the terrace with its imposing balusters. The palace has now been turned into a college, and nothing remains of the darbarhall, once famous for its oil paintings on canvas depicting various Indian scenes, and rows of chandeliers interspersed with cut crystal balls, which gave the

hall a dazzling effect rather like the Sheesh mahals of Rajasthan, the Aina mahal of Bhuj, or the mirror room of Wadhwan. The living quarters of the maharana and his family, the halls that once hosted great dinners and parties and the darbarhall where audiences were held, are now classrooms, libraries, offices and assembly halls. From the sea, the palace looks like an Italian villa.

In the same year, HH Maharana Bhav Sinhji built the Huzoor palace, with its impressive domes, and equipped Porbandar with schools, temples and other facilities. Over the next two decades, he built bridges, roads, reservoirs, and commissioned a project to convert the salt marshes into freshwater sources.

HH Maharana Bhav Sinhji was succeeded by his son HH Maharana Natwarsinhji in 1908AD, when he was just seven years old. He became a great cricketer; he was the first to captain India on an overseas tour to England in 1932AD, and in 1946AD started the Duleep School of Cricket, which is held in high esteem throughout Asia. It was HH Maharana Natwarsinhji who, upon achieving his majority at the age of eighteen, went to work immediately to begin the modernisation of Porbandar on a grand scale. He was a patron of Indian literature, music and the nationalist movement. During his rule, Ravindranath Tagore, the Indian Nobel Prize winning poet, visited Porbandar in 1923AD, and Mahatma Gandhi visited

EUROPEAN STYLE SCULPTURE AT THE ANANT NIWAS, KHAMBALA

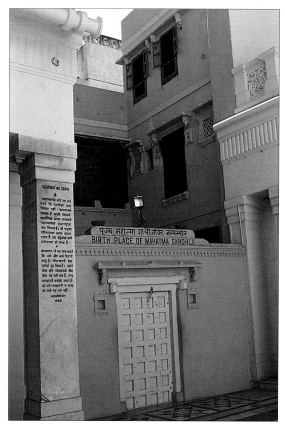

THE DIWAN BUNGALOW OF PORBANDAR, WHERE MAHATMA GANDHI WAS BORN

HH MAHARANA NATWARSINHJI, INDIA'S FIRST TEST CRICKET CAPTAIN

his birthplace in 1928AD. He encouraged artists like Narayan Kher and poets, and in later years started a nationalist movement by promoting Indian literature at a time when most Indian princes prided themselves on their familiarity with English literature.

He moved his residence to the Huzoor palace, a massive structure reminiscent of a European mansion, sprawling within large grounds at the very edge of the sea. The palace has various wings in a zigzag formation, which make for numerous forecourts and rear courtyards, with gardens and fountains carefully and attractively arranged. The structure is in a very modern style, crowned by trussed timber roofs and balustraded terraces offering extensive views of the beach and the sea. Semi-circular porticos on neo-Classical pillars offer entry to the palace from different sides. Huge chandeliers and crystal light fittings illuminate the dining and drawing rooms, some of which have colourful Italian tiles, fine furniture, paintings, porcelain vases and old fireplaces. The reception is reached through rooms hung with portraits of the royal family, and historic photographs of weddings, events, gatherings, a lion shoot in Gir and of the family. The old reception hall has a Gir lion and European style statues pointing the way towards a substantial wooden staircase with slim, carved balusters, illuminated by crystal lamps in brass stands, connected by concealed wiring switchboards to ensure that the beauty of the staircases is not marred by exposed wiring. The games room displays marine paintings by Juan Couver and a billiard table. Another hallway has a piano, reminiscent of the days when HH Maharana Natwarsinhji composed European style music, patronized artists and himself took an interest in architectural designs. The zanana has a banqueting hall displaying silverware and pleasant galleries. The library has huge mahogany cabinets housing works by European and Indian writers, including Galworthy and Hood classics. The main drawing room, which once saw the reception of important guests, has as the centrepiece a beautiful fountain feeding a pleasure pool, colourful Italian tiled floors, white colonnades and intricate furniture. The contours of the palace walls, with Classical balustrades and Grecian style urns, yield to lovely white sanded beaches and the sea.

A short distance from Porbandar, near the site of the Khambala dam, HH Maharana Natwarsinhji saw the perfect setting for a mansion retreat. The building was named Anant niwas – after his European wife who was given the Indian name of Anant Kunverba – and is in the European style with sloping timber roofs. The Anant niwas is entered through huge wrought iron gates, bearing a monogram of the Hindu god, Lord Hanuman, and a path sloping toward the portico goes past a small garden.

The once formal gardens are on various levels, with balustraded steps going down to lower lawns, with the lawns at the bottom having covered enclosures for Italian statues. The portico in the front has steps leading to a doorway flanked by two dolphins.

The interiors are appointed in original furniture from the early-20th century AD Art Nouveau and Art Deco styles, and have Art Deco bathrooms to match. The drawing room has an interesting painting of HH Maharana Natwarsinhji on jute in a gilt frame, Art Deco furnishings and Art Deco objects in glass and ceramics in a glass cabinet, ceramic vases, and old photographs of HH Maharana Natwarsinhji and his European wife, and of the royal family of Limbdi.

Next door is a room with an old wind-up HMV gramophone, cabinets that housed the family's record collection, portraits of Maharana Bhav Sinhji and of his wife, and European landscape paintings. The banqueting room, appointed in Art Deco style, has chairs with built-in ash trays. The rooms surround a courtyard with timber roofs and nine inch square darkly coloured Italian tiles make up the floor. The library stocks works by John Buchan, Georgette Heyer, Edgar Wallace and Dennis Robbins, all in heavy wooden cabinets.

The maharana's bedroom with Art Deco furniture and en suite lilac bathroom, the maharani's room with its pink bathroom, the guest rooms in orange, the morning room and the children's room with a crib-like bed – all are retained in original condition. A spiral staircase takes one down to the

THE MEMORIAL TO MAHATMA GANDHI WITH PAINTINGS BY NARAYAN KHER, THE PATRON PAINTER OF THE ROYAL FAMILY OF PORBANDAR

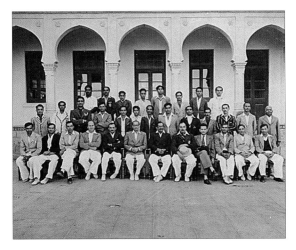

HH MAHARANA NATWARSINHJI'S CRICKET TEAM SELECTED TO REPRESENT INDIA

Porbandar

treasure room, with its heavy safes and wooden cupboards. Every room, window and gallery brings in extensive views of the well wooded Barda hills, and there are good views of Khambala lake, too.

On the opposite side of the dam are the maharana's private orchards of mango and other fruit, and the old orchard bungalow is now inhabited by a Nathani family which served the royal family for several generations.

HH Maharana Natwarsinhji died in 1979AD, leaving no heir, his only son, Yuvraj Udaimansinhji, having predeceased him in 1977AD. Thus ended a clan that had seen some 2,000 years of recorded history, during which it had won honours in every human activity, from battle to literature and music, and from architecture to sport. Locals believe that its eventual downfall was the result of a curse placed on the ancestral family by Santokben, a woman who

believed herself to have been wronged in the royal court.

The palaces of Porbandar are now owned by HH Maharana Harendra de Silva QC, HH Maharana Natwarsinhji's stepson. Harendra lives and works in London. He is a Queen's Counsel, a part time judge and a keen golfer. A thoroughly affable character, with two children, Ayesha and Nihal, he visits Porbandar frequently.

SUNDAMAPURI TEMPLE AT PORBANDAR

ANANT NIWAS AT KHAMBALA

The Princely State of Rajkot

**9 GUN
SALUTE STATE**

Rajkot was a Jadeja Rajput state, founded in the early-17th century AD by Vibhoji, who received from his uncle, the Jam Saheb of Nawanagar (present-day Jamnagar), an estate as his share of the kingdom of Nawanagar upon the death of his father, Ajoji, at the historic battle of Bhuchar Mori between Nawanagar and the Muslim invaders. Vibhoji married the Vaghela Princess of Sardhar, and inherited the fiefdom of Sardhar.

Many are the tales of Vibhoji's valour. He supported the Mughal prince and heir to the Mughal empire, Shah Jahan, in his efforts to vanquish the Vaghela Rajputs, who had become a thorn in the side of the Mughals in Gujarat, killing in battle the leader of the Vaghela clan, Kanoji. Vibhoji's son, Maheramanaji, succeeded him in 1635AD, and helped the Mughal empire once again, this time to suppress revolts by Kathi chieftains, and in return received additional estates and villages from Azam Khan, the governor of Gujarat. He made his own son, Sahebji, the thanedar of Sardhar. During his rule, his younger brother, Mota Kumbhaji, separated from the family and founded his own chiefdom at Ardoi, later to become the princely state of Gondal.

Rajkot was conquered by his successor, Bamanioji, who died in 1695AD in battle, and it was left to Bamanioji's son, Meramanaji, to take over as ruler of Rajkot; the latter brought both Rajkot and its surrounding villages under control in 1707AD, following the death of the Mughal emperor, Aurangzeb, and the weakening generally of Mughal influence in the area.

But Meramanaji's success was shortlived. Rajkot was seized by the governor of the Mughal empire at

RANJIT VILAS PALACE

Junagadh in 1720AD, and the fortified walls of Rajkot were built by Masum Khan of Junagadh in 1722AD. Skirmishes continued, and Rajkot and Sardhar often changed hands. Meramanji, who came to the throne in the late-18th century AD, was a great poet and the author of Pravin sagar, a classic Hindi epic, and a good administrator. Captain Ballantyne, the first British resident of Rajkot, restored the entire state of Rajkot-Sardhar to Meramanji's son and successor, Ranmalji the second, in 1822AD. Meramanaji the fourth was honoured by the British government for abolishing female infanticide in 1857AD.

During the late-19th and early-20th centuries AD, Rajkot achieved considerable prominence as the capital of the Kathiawadi peninsula. Alfred High School, an English school, was founded in 1853AD, Hunter Training College for men and Barton Training College for women teachers were established in Rajkot, and Rajkumar College, an English public school for princes, British officers' children and the upper caste Indian society, was established in Gujarat, along the lines of the public schools of Eton and Harrow.

Karsandas, a social reformer, and Karamchand Gandhi, the father of Mahatma Gandhi, who had earlier served as diwan of Kutch, were appointed to look after affairs of state. In 1923AD, during the rule of HH Thakore Saheb Lakdiraj Sinhji, known as a liberal ruler, the Kathiawad Rajakiva parishad was

held, a seminar for princes and prominent persons of Saurashtra. Rajkot Praja Pratinidhi Sabha, the citizens' council, was founded during his rule in September 1925AD; the Dharma Sabha, the justice council, was inaugurated shortly afterwards, and so too the Khedut Maha Sabha, the farmers' council. His rule saw Ravindranath Tagore, the Indian Nobel Prize winning poet, visit Rajkot, and Jawaharlal Nehru was welcomed warmly to a youth conference in 1929AD.

But HH Thakore Saheb Dharmendra Sinhji, who came to the throne after HH Thakore Saheb Lakhajiraj Sinhji in 1930AD, presented a complete contrast to his liberal father. He taxed the people heavily, hoarded sugar, matches and other necessities for blackmarket operations during times of shortage, encouraged gambling, and spent 50% of the state's income on his personal pleasures and vices. There was satyagraha in Rajkot in 1938-39AD, with the citizens protesting against their tyrannical ruler, and indeed no real progress took place in Rajkot during his rule. It was left to HH Thakore Saheb Prahlad Sinhji, who came to the throne upon HH Thakore Saheb Dharmendra Sinhji's death, to try and make amends.

The present owner of the palaces of Rajkot is Thakore Saheb Manohar Sinhji, who studied management in England. A well known politician, he is a member of the Congress Party and has represented Rajkot in the legislative assembly and at

cabinet level. His son, Yuvraj Mandatta Sinh, is an entrepreneur involved in a number of successful ventures.

The present residence of the royal family of Rajkot is the Ranjit vilas palace. The palace is built in the Indo-European style, with Italianesque fountains in the forecourt, cusped arches, Venetian-Gothic arched windows and carved jarokha balconies. The rear courtyard has a domed and pillared biradari. The interiors have been well maintained with a mixture of fixtures and furnishings both old and new. Some parts of the palace now house offices of the family businesses. The family's country house, on the shores of lake Randharda, may be opened as a resort soon.

The older darbargadh of the royal family of Rajkot can still be seen at Sardhar, and is owned by the same family. Enclosing a substantial group of buildings and courtyards, the palace's medieval fort walls rise up beside a picturesque lake.

The Princely State of Rajpipla

**13 GUN
SALUTE STATE**

The princely state of Rajpipla, formerly known as Nandod or Nanded, was situated in the foothills of the Satpura mountain range, an area of outstanding natural beauty between two important rivers of western India, the Narmada and the Tapti.

The state spanned over 1,500 square miles, of which 600 square miles were forests, and the rest fertile agricultural plains and river valleys. It grew to be one of the most prosperous princely states in Gujarat, second indeed only to Baroda, with a salute of thirteen guns. Yet, prior to the 12th century AD, Rajpipla had been an almost unknown little principality of the Vasavada dynasty, surrounded by dense jungle.

The history of Rajpipla changed when Chokrana, a Parmara Rajput prince of Ujjain in Malwa (now the western part of the state of Madya Pradesh), settled in the town of Rajpipla following disputes with his father. His daughter was married to the Gohil Rajput king Mokhadaji of Ghogha, whose descendants became the rulers of Bhavnagar, and when Chokrana died without an heir, Samar Sinhji, the son of Mokhadaji, succeeded to the throne and

changed his name to Arjun Sinhji. From that time, Rajpipla was ruled by the Gohil Rajput dynasty.

Times were turbulent, and it was not easy for the Gohils to retain their territory. Gemal Sinhji, one of the successors of Samar Sinhji, had his capital invaded by Sultan Ahmed Shah in 1413AD. After Gemal Sinhji's death in 1421AD, his son Vijaypat sought the help of the hill tribals, the Bhils, to recover the territories lost to the sultan. Vijaypat's son, Hari Sinh, once again faced invasion from Sultan Ahmed Shah and deserted Rajpipla. He became an outlaw for twelve years before recovering his kingdom from the sultan in the 1440s AD. By the mid-16th century AD, the Gohil dynasty had become quite strong. It is said that even Maharana Udai Sinhji, the powerful Gohil Rajput ruler of Mewar, had to take refuge in the Rajpipla hills following the taking of his fort palace by the Mughal emperor Akhbar at Chittor, and before he founded the city of Udaipur and made it the capital of Mewar.

In 1573AD, Emperor Akhbar had to establish an outpost near Rajpipla to check revolts by the Gohil Rajputs, and the Gohil king Pritviraj Sinhji often had to seek refuge in the hills when his revolts were

WALL PAINTING BY THE EUROPEAN ARTIST, WALI, IN THE NATWAR NIWAS PALACE

FRONT ELEVATION OF THE VIJAY PALACE

DISPLAY OF ROYAL WARDROBE IN THE VIJAY PALACE MUSEUM

POLO AND RACING WERE THE PRIME INTERESTS OF HH MAHARAJAH VIJAY SINHJI IN THE 1930s AD

FOYER OF THE VIJAY PALACE

Rajpipla

TEMPLE TO THE DEITY OF THE MAHARAJAHS OF RAJPIPLA

crushed by the Mughals. In 1594AD, Pritviraj Sinhji gave refuge to Sultan Muzzaffar Shah, the last of the Gujarat sultanate, an act that particularly angered Akhbar, who set upon Rajpipla. The Mughals, still powerful during this period, soon put the king in his place, increasing his tribute to Rs.35,556/- and securing an undertaking that Rajpipla would provide 1,000 men for the Mughal army.

In 1705AD, the Mughal emperor Aurangazeb sent a contingent from Delhi to fight the Marathas in southern Gujarat, for they had begun to emerge as a powerful force in India, weakening the Mughal power south of Delhi. Verisal, the King of Nandod-Rajpipla, refused to assist and instead plundered the Mughal territories of Gujarat.

In 1715AD, the Mughal empire had begun to weaken still further, and Verisal's successor, Jeet Sinhji, took over his entire ancestral territory and made Rajpipla his capital in 1730AD after forging a treaty with the powerful Gaekwads of Baroda. But his successors had problems with the Gaekwads, until a daughter of a Rajpipla king was married to Damaji Gaekwad, and the tribute was partially reduced. Internal disputes and family feuds continued, and the Gaekwads and the British were called in to arbitrate. Nahar Sinhji was appointed ruler in 1793AD by the British agent, Willoughby.

The early-19th century AD saw a decline in the power of the Rajpipla rulers, principally because of revolts by the Bhils, until agreements with the British crown by Verisal the second in 1821AD brought some degree of peace to Rajpipla. The Bhils were crushed in 1860AD, and Raja Gambhir Sinhji received a salute of eleven guns in 1860AD. Due to alleged mismanagement, the British intervened in the administration of Rajpipla in the 1880s AD and 1890s AD.

Rajpipla first caught sight of power and prosperity when HH Maharajah Chattra Sinhji came to the throne in 1897AD, and set Rajpipla on a progressive path. But the builder of modern and affluent Rajpipla was his son, HH Maharajah Vijay Sinhji, who ascended to the throne in 1915AD and proved to be a great administrator. On him was conferred the title of Knight Commander, the hereditary title of the maharajahs, and the gun salutes for the ruler of Rajpipla were increased from eleven to thirteen.

During his rule, Rajpipla introduced high schools, ninety-three primary schools, including seven English schools, and numerous privately run classes. Primary education was free and high school fees nominal. A number of scholarships were introduced to encourage high school education in the state, and even collegiate-technical education elsewhere, for students of Rajpipla. There was a large hospital, five dispensaries and a veterinary hospital in the state, good public works, a criminal and a civil court, good roads, a forty mile railway line connecting Rajpipla to Ankleshwar – a junction on the Delhi-Ahmedabad-Bombay line – together with a nineteen mile steam railroad and tramway connecting towns along the river Narmada with villages in the interior, and a power station supplying electricity and a pump station supplying water to the

NATWAR NIWAS PALACE

Rajpipla

town. The revenue of the state increased from Rs.13 lakhs to Rs.27 lakhs per annum between 1915-30AD, and is said to have reached Rs.36 lakhs in 1948AD, though taxes were actually reduced in percentage terms! HH Maharajah Vijay Sinhji regularised the land revenue systems, introduced pensions for public servants, and increased the salaries of the police and military. His relief efforts during droughts and floods were appreciated. He took an interest in agriculture, and improved the quality of cotton, grain and fruit grown in his territory. Town planning in 1927AD was far-sighted, building permission being granted subject to three or four feet of space being left available for subsequent road widening. New buildings were designed to be well integrated and harmonious.

Sport was HH Maharajah Vijay Sinhji's passion. He was a keen horseman, and maintained one of the finest stables of race horses in India. His horse, Embargo, won the Irish Derby in 1926AD and the Belgian Grand Prix in 1927AD, and another horse, Windsor Lad, won the Epsom Derby in 1934AD. Other horses, like Melesigenes, won him almost every prize worth its name in races at Bombay, Pune and other Indian courses, and in 1932-33AD he was India's foremost owner. Though spending much of the sporting season in England, he would return to India in winter when he encouraged outdoor sports like football, hockey and cricket. Sport was made compulsory for students of Rajpipla state. He

equipped Rajpipla with a polo ground and gymkhana club. Rajpipla's joining the Indian Union in 1947AD, however, put paid to one of the maharajah's dreams for Rajpipla, a 150 acre aerodrome – it was never built.

Surprisingly, HH Maharajah Vijay Sinhji, who was known for his lengthy sojourns in Europe and his loyalty to the British crown, started a nationalist movement in the 1940s AD and, like his fellow Gohil Rajput rulers in Bhavnagar and Udaipur, was one of the first princes to hand over his state to the Indian Union, along with Rs.28 lakhs lying in the state treasury. At a meeting in his Nepean Sea Road residence in Bombay, he urged other rulers to give up their states in the cause of a united nation. He died at his manor house in Windsor, England, in 1951AD but was cremated at Rampura, on the banks of the river Narmada, eighteen kilometres from his former capital.

The oldest palace of Rajpipla is the Chattra vilas, the royal palace of HH Maharajah Chattra Sinhji. The palace is in a typical European style, with oriel windows and Italian features, and the darbarhall is in an outhouse, resembling a Gothic church. Inside, the darbarhall has carved wooden brackets, supporting galleries and balconies, but is otherwise empty. The palace itself is now a college, but is rather dilapidated.

HH Maharajah Chattra Sinhji built separate palaces for his four sons, of which the best

FOUNTAIN IN THE DRAWING ROOM OF THE NATWAR NIWAS PALACE

REAR VIEW OF THE VIJAY PALACE

A WALL PAINTING OF LORD KRISHNA AT THE NATWAR NIWAS PALACE

ROYAL WEDDING PROCESSION

maintained is the Vijay palace, built for crown prince Maharajah Vijay Sinhji in 1915AD. The palace looks rather like a villa in Italy, with an Italianesque fountain surrounded by palms in the forecourt, a Classical colonnaded semi-circular portico as the entrance, together with Corinthian pillars, Gothic arches, European domes and views of the river at the rear.

It is now an hotel owned by the royal family and run by staff, with twenty-two rooms spread amongst the main building and the numerous outhouses – the old guesthouse, garden bungalow and staff quarters. The seven acre grounds have been laid into formal gardens by a professional landscape architect.

Crested arch doors lead to a marble floored hall, which now serves as the reception of the hotel. The drawing room has retained its original character, with European settees, elegant tables, royal portraits and black metal European statues. The banqueting hall, next to the drawing room, has a long wooden communal dining table, twenty-four carved wooden chairs and a wall spanned by historic photographs of HH Maharajah Vijay Sinhji's exploits on the race track. Numerous objects, old and new, and utensils in brass, marble and ceramics, decorate the hall. A portable screen separates the banqueting and drawing areas, and this is removed when the palace is chartered for corporate conferences. The suites and rooms have been appointed with original French and other European furniture from the palace and from the royal railway saloon carriage, long sold, and with cane and bamboo furniture from the royal tents, which were used by HH Maharajah Vijay Sinhji on his shooting camps, for which guests from various princely states would assemble in the reserve forests of Rajpipla; the bathrooms and toilets, however, have modern fixtures.

A part of the palace now forms a museum, displaying the maharajah's personal collection of richly embroidered royal attire – some of it bearing the original crest of Rajpipla – crockery, glass and crystalware, paintings, portraits and stuffed animals. Hunting trophies from the palace are now to be found in the museum. The palace had a family pool near the entrance, but this has now been filled in, and, to respect the privacy of hotel residents, a new pool has been created to the rear of the palace, with wrought iron seating facing banana plantations and the river Karjan. The outhouse of the palace has a dining hall with a long banqueting table, elegant chairs and a row of convex mirrors, each of which reflects the entire table in miniature!

Beside the hall is a modern air conditioned restaurant for hotel guests. Near the palace is a gymkhana, offering a variety of outdoor sports.

HH Maharajah Raghuvir Sinhji, the present owner of the Vijay palace, received his bachelors degree from Pune in 1963AD, and subsequently obtained diplomas in management and law. He was made Knight Commander in Vilnius, Belorusse in 1980AD, and a Knight of Justice in Poland in the same year; he was honoured by the Commonwealth of Kentucky in 1981AD, and in 1982AD was given the Knight Order of St George, and made Honorary Consul to Barbados, in Bombay, a position which he still holds today. He married Rukmani Devi, a princess from Jaisalmer, in 1964AD, a wedding reported in great detail by National Geographic magazine. Maharani Rukmani Devi has a postgraduate degree and joined her husband on his many travels abroad, before settling with him in Bombay and Rajpipla.

"The abolition of privy purses was inevitable, but it did come as a shock and many royals were unable to cope with the change. Most of our Rajput community had never been involved in business, and were too proud to take up employment," explains Maharani Rukmani Devi, "but I feel most members

VADIA PALACE BUILT IN THE 1930S AD, IN THE INDO-SARACENIC STYLE

MAHARANI RUKMANI DEVI IN TRADITIONAL RAJPUT ATTIRE

of our community perhaps spend too much time complaining, instead of doing something about their plight. Take the Sindhi community, for example. It lost everything during the India-Pakistan partition, land, houses, businesses, but the people worked hard and some of them have made it big. We accepted the change and opened our palace as an hotel in the early-1970s AD. There was no real tourism then, and we usually rented the whole palace out to film shooting crews.

"Over the last twenty-five years, more than 160 different Hindi feature films, Gujarati feature films, TV series and advertisements have been shot at Rajpipla, with the Vijay palace as one of the locations. Thanks to our palace, Rajpipla is called the Hollywood of Gujarat. Had we worked on it earlier, we should have diversified into studios and things like that, but now the big studios are at Halol, forty kilometres from here, and most of the Gujarati films are shot there.

"In the 1980s AD, business came because of the Sardar Sarovar dam. There were engineers, financiers and environmentalists, for and against the dam, visiting Rajpipla. Many multinationals and large Indian corporates have opened textile, petrochemical and other industries in the vicinity of Rajpipla, and we get a number of executives and engineers staying with us. Weekend traffic from Baroda is good, too. We have hosted many conferences and weddings.

"My husband invested in real estate in Bombay, and was a partner in projects of the Raheja family, who are big land developers in Bombay, including cinemas. His hobbies were painting and sport, but he does not indulge in them much these days," she continues. "I was involved in politics in the 1980s AD and was a member of the Congress party before joining Bharatiya Janata Party. I lost interest in politics at the beginning of this decade and instead took an interest in this hotel," she says, "and now our plans are to organise the hotel properly, improve the facilities and renovate twenty to twenty-five more rooms, once our own bungalow is ready outside the premises, and we can move out."

The maharani continues: "I travelled extensively with my husband, but I still rate India as the best place to see, and I am quite bored with international travel now, especially since becoming a vegetarian. I think Indian cuisine offers the world's best vegetarian food. Rajasthan is my favourite destination – perhaps it's an inherent love for my native place. I think Rajasthan is very romantic, and I'm very keen on Rajput culture and Rajasthani

CHATTRA NIWAS PALACE, THE OLDEST PALACE OF RAJPIPLA

clothes," she goes on. "Varanasi is another place I don't mind visiting over and over again. We live in Bombay, because of my son's education and because, before our hotel really picked up, there was little to do here, but now we've started spending time in Rajpipla because of the hotel. I am not very fond of Bombay, but I do acknowledge the opportunities offered by large cities. I prefer Delhi, and I have my own house there. But, for the princes of Gujarat, Bombay was nearer, and most big states of Gujarat had Bombay residences. I love writing and reading Hindi devotional and romantic poetry. Music is another passion – I have learnt Indian classical music and I sing. Some of my accompanyist instruments are in our private museum, but my very personal ones I keep in my rooms. I am publishing a book of the poems and compositions of my guru, and of my own work."

HH Maharajah Raghuvir Sinhji adds: "I am opening a cultural centre and tribal museum near the palace gate, for which I have got some financial assistance from the Indian government. Besides tribal artefacts, utensils, handcraft and folk objects, we are planning to recreate our coronation room, which will house our royal throne and ceremonial objects, instead of their being in the small palace museum here. Rajpipla is due for a museum now, and we have suggested to the government that the school in Chattra vilas palace be relocated, and the palace converted into a museum. We have custody of

HH Maharajah Raghuvir Sinhji of Rajpipla, on his wedding day in 1964AD

the darbarhall, which has some good wood carvings inside."

Yuvraj Manvendar Sinhji, their son and the heir to the palace, went to Bombay Scottish School and Bombay University, where he studied commerce at Mithibhai College. "I am very keen on agriculture and am trying to promote organic, sustainable farming – involving vermiculture and with no pesticides or chemical fertilizers. I have mango orchards and a farm by the river Narmada," says

Yuvraj Manvendar Sinhji, "but as the palace hotel is doing well, I am thinking of opening an eco-friendly resort in the seven acre palace complex with organically home-grown vegetables."

Another of the other three palaces created for HH Maharajah Chattra Sinhji's sons, built for HH Maharajah Natwar Sinhji, is the Natwar niwas palace, now rather dilapidated outside, but well maintained within. The reception room has an Italian marble-statued fountain inset into an Italian marble floor, a dome inlaid with stained glass, Corinthian pillars and a wall hung with friezes of events from Lord Krishna's life by an Italian artist, Wali, who took refuge in Rajpipla during World War II. Another sitting room has a huge chandelier, period furniture and a wall painting of Maharana Pratap, the great war hero of 16th century AD Rajasthan and a member of the same Gohil Rajput clan as the maharajahs of Rajpipla, framed by semi-circular Corinthian columns projecting from the wall. Another drawing room has an equally impressive wall painting of Shivaji, the Maratha king who initiated the rise of the Marathas as a major national force in India, and who plundered the Mughal armies. The dining hall has a long banqueting table and carved chairs.

Leading to the first floor is a massive balustraded wooden staircase: its crystal light fitting has concealed switches, and no exposed wiring to mar the beauty of the woodwork. The upper storey of the palace has been rented to a day school, and the downstairs section has been retained by Rani Hemlata Devi, the present owner of the palace, and who is married to the Rao Saheb of Poshina.

The finest palace of Rajpipla is the Indrajeet Padmini mahal, better known as the Vadia palace, as the entire population of Vadia was relocated and the village demolished to enable the palace to be built there in the 1930s AD. The palace was set in a 151 acre estate, with well laid out formal gardens and mango and lime orchards, and the building itself covered almost an acre (4,320 square yards). It was financed by HH Maharajah Vijay Sinhji's winnings at the Epsom Derby, and cost around Rs.40 lakhs. Surprisingly, the architecture is Indo-Saracenic, a blend of the Hindu and Islamic styles, rather than European, though there are some elements of European influence there, and this despite the fashion for Venetian-Gothic architecture in that period, the maharajah's long stays in England, and the work being commissioned to Shapoorji Curimbouy & Co., a firm of the Zoroastrian Parsee community which, in spite of a Persian ancestry, prided itself on being very European. The palace is dominated by a huge dome, flanked by smaller domes, and an umbrella dome of the kind you see in the palaces of Jaipur and Bikaner, together with side turrets at either end, crowned by cupolas. The massive porticos at the front, rear and side entrances are supported by cusped arches in the Indo-Saracenic

tradition. Arches run the length of the front elevation, and, to the rear, intricate lattice-work on stone probably protected the royal family from prying eyes.

The interior, however, retains much of the European character one would expect from a palace erected during the 1930s AD. Much of the flooring is in Italian marble, of different colours and arranged in various geometric patterns, such that no two rooms or galleries are floored alike. At the rear is a marble fountain, with intricate patterns matching the flooring of the gallery in which it is situated. The thousand or so doors and wooden windows of the palace were made from Burmese teak. The palace was centrally air conditioned, with ducts still visible on the walls. It had eleven bedrooms – nine distributed in the two storeys of the palace, a subterranean chamber and a suite facing the terrace – all with bathrooms attached. The ballroom had Burmese teak flooring, the sitting room was adorned with wall paintings depicting dancing girls, and the bar room walls were hung with pictures of intoxicated monkeys; while the drawing room had beautiful paintings of events from Lord Krishna's life, the prayer room had a series of wall and ceiling frescos of Hindu deities, while the receiving hall behind the portico was painted with floral and faunal subjects. As at the Natwar niwas, the painting was done by the Italian artist, Wali, yet the quality of Indian devotional paintings and other local themes is

FLORAL PAINTING IN A BEDROOM AT THE NATWAR NIWAS PALACE

A WALL PAINTING OF SHIVAJI, THE 17TH CENTURY AD MARATHA CHIEFTAIN, AT NATWAR NIWAS

PRINCESS MOHINI KUAR, DAUGHTER OF HH MAHARAJAH VIJAY SINHJI, SHARED HER FATHER'S PASSION FOR HORSES

flawless. The drawing room was illuminated by lights concealed in marble globes, the latter filled also with exotic perfumes: a water circulation system enabled the marble globes to revolve, so that the scent of the perfumes spread throughout the hall. Two elevators carried the royal family and their guests to the first floor. The kitchen was in an outhouse, partially below ground so that it did not spoil the view from the galleries or the view of the intricate rear facade of the palace. Along a thirty yard long underground and insulated passage, food was conveyed on trolleys to the pantry in the main building.

The palace was inherited in 1951AD by the maharajah's younger son, HH Maharajah Kumar Indrajeet Sinhji. The palace is now the Forest Ranger's College: the formal gardens, where fountains once played, are plantations; the bedrooms and sitting rooms are classrooms and offices; and a large hall houses a natural history museum. Some of the downstair rooms form the collector's office. The outhouses play home to an Ayurvedic herbal medicine centre started in the 1970s AD. The park-like grounds are now a concrete jungle of modern residential quarters for government staff, and buildings housing government offices.

FRONT ENTRANCE TO THE VIJAY PALACE

The Princely State of Wadhwan

**9 GUN
SALUTE STATE**

The rulers of Wadhwan, like those of Wankaner, Dhrangadhra and Limbdi, at whose states we look in other chapters, were members of the Jhala Rajput clan which came to Gujarat from Sindh in the 12th century AD, settling first at Patdi, and then moving to Halwad following skirmishes with the Muslims in the second half of the 15th century AD.

There are conflicting reports about whether the Wadhwan clan separated directly from the elder Jhala clan at Halwad in the 15th century AD, or whether they separated from the Wankaner branch of the clan in the 17th century AD.

The best known of the Wadhwan rulers were the brothers HH Thakore Saheb Dajiraj Sinhji and HH Thakore Saheb Bal Sinhji, the first of whom ruled for just three years in the late-19th century AD before his death at the age of twenty-one, when the administration passed to his brother. HH Thakore Saheb Dajiraj Sinhji was a widely travelled man, married to the Princess of Vizakapatnam, and had brought a number of acquisitions from Europe. Until then, the rulers of Wadhwan, like other rulers, had reigned from a darbargadh, the system of town

THE SUMPTUOUS BAL VILAS PALACE DARBARHALL WITH A COLLECTION OF VERY FINE EUROPEAN AND INDIAN FURNITURE

ENTRANCE GATE TO THE BAL VILAS PALACE

palaces that prevailed in Gujarat, but, as had become the practice among rulers, he moved away from the town, setting up two palaces; a lake palace, surrounded by the Surendranagar reservoir, and the Rajmahal palace, which served initially as a European guesthouse and residency. Unfortunately, the lake palace was left incomplete, but the Rajmahal was completed by HH Thakore Saheb Bal Sinhji, and decorated by the acquisitions of both brothers. It was later named Bal vilas palace, after HH Thakore Saheb Bal Sinhji, and is now the royal residence.

The two brothers introduced a wide range of reforms and public services, including schools and hospitals, and their good work was continued by

HH Thakore Saheb Jaswant Sinhji, by HH Thakore Saheb Zoravar Sinhji, and finally by HH Maharajah Surendra Sinhji, and it was the last who signed the agreements leading to Indian Union. The new district capital of Surendranagar, now a major industrial and administrative town of Gujarat, was named after him. HH Maharajah Surendra Sinhji, who went to school in England, had a private governor, Mr Mayer of Millfield. The families of the princely states of Dhrangadhra, Shahpura and Wadhwan bought a country estate in England, where the princes lived during the holidays away from their respective boarding schools. The house was left to Mr Mayer once they had completed their

education and returned to India.

HH Maharajah Surendra Sinhji learnt administration in the court of Wankaner, where he spent eighteen years during the reigns of HH Maharajah Bane Sinhji and HH Maharajah Amar Sinhji. In 1951AD, HH Maharajah Surendra Sinhji moved for a year to Bombay, and then to Bangalore, where his son and heir, Yuvraj Chaitanya Dev Sinhji, went to school at Bishop's Cotton and St Joseph's.

HH Maharajah Chaitanya Dev Sinhji is a keen car enthusiast, and raced various sports cars between 1973AD and 1983AD. His interest in vintage cars encouraged further research, and many of the old cars in his and other royal families' possession have

INNER COURTYARD OF THE BAL VILAS PALACE

CEILING OF THE BAL VILAS PALACE DARBARHALL, WITH HIGHLY DETAILED GILTWORK AND PAINTED CORNICE WORK CONTAINING FURTHER ELABORATE DECORATIVE PANELS

THRONE AND PORTRAITS OF THE RULERS OF WADHWAN AT THE BAL VILAS PALACE

Wadhwan

UNIQUE FRENCH VELVET CURTAINS COVER THE DOORWAY TO THE BILLIARD ROOM AT THE BAL VILAS PALACE

leads to what are now the family's quarters when they come to Wadhwan from Bangalore. In the centre is a courtyard of the grandest scale in Gujarat, with a beautiful pool, surrounded by intricate Rajput pillars, and with an angel as the centrepiece. Around the pool are marble biradaris. Models of palaces, and a painting of the Hawa mahal, stand in different corners of the courtyard.

The courtyard offers access to the darbarhall, which is on a majestic scale, enclosed by columns with vase and pillar bases meeting in intricate cusped arches, and crowned by a beautiful ceiling decorated with European paintings and giltwork. The windows are curtained with velvet. "It is said that HH Thakore Saheb Dajiraj Sinhji bought an entire velvet factory in France, and after the velvet for the palace was woven, the factory was closed down so that the designs of the velvet curtains, tapestry and upholstery could never be repeated," says HH Maharajah Chaitanya Dev Sinhji. "My father worked hard at maintaining the palaces, but after the privy purse was abolished, he just gave up. Now my son, Yuvraj Sidharth Sinhji, is keen on hotels and catering, and we are doing up the palace as an Heritage Hotel. He is thinking of going to catering school, which would be useful for running the hotel."

The walls of the darbarhall are lined with historic portraits. On an exotically carpeted mandap are a canopied throne for the king, and seating for his

THE CANOPIED THRONE OF THE MAHARAJAH AT THE BAL VILAS PALACE

been sympathetically restored to their former glory.

The drive to the Bal vilas palace takes you through grounds that extend to some fourteen acres, with a cricket pitch, tennis courts, old fountains and small, now dry, ponds in floral shapes which once supported lotuses and other lilies. At the northern and southern entrances are huge porticos with archways, and the eastern and western facades have galleries of stepped arches. A huge wooden staircase

heirs and advisers. Next to the darbarhall is the hall of mirrors from various countries in Europe, now used as the family's prayer room. The billiard room has beautiful ceiling decorations. It is said that artists were brought in from France to paint the room, but they had only completed the ceiling before the ruler, who had commissioned the work, died. The drawing room, beside the darbarhall, once boasted a huge punkah, made from cut crystal, which has been converted into a lampstand; a crystal hookah, fine upholstered chairs and a rich carpet. A gilded throne occupies one of the rooms around the darbarhall.

Outside the palace is the garage, where HH Maharajah Chaitanya Dev Sinhji pursues his hobby of restoring motor cars. His own collection includes a 1918AD Crossley, perhaps the last surviving example in the world today; a 1936AD Mercedes 7-seater convertible; a 1947AD Lincoln; Buicks from 1944AD and 1947AD, and some more recent sports models, supplemented from time to time by cars from friends and fellow royals which he may have undertaken to restore.

THE CARD ROOM AT THE BAL VILAS PALACE

POOL AT THE BAL VILAS PALACE WITH AN ANGEL IN THE INNER COURTYARD SURROUNDED BY ORNATE RAJPUT PILLARS DECORATED IN ORIGINAL COLOURS

The Princely State of Wankaner

11 GUN SALUTE STATE

Wankaner in Gujarati means the bend of a river – an appropriate name for a township located on the banks of the river Machchu, in an area comprising a tract of rolling hills separating the plains of Kathiawad from the flat desert wilderness of the Little Rann of Kutch. Driving through the barren countryside of broken scrub, it is hard to imagine that Wankaner was once an important princely state of Saurashtra, the land of over 200 rulers: and possesses one of the grandest palaces in Gujarat, perhaps among the finest in all of India!

Like Dhrangadhra, Wankaner was ruled by the clan of Jhala Rajputs who came to Saurashtra from Sindh in the early years of the 12th century AD. The Jhalas are said to have been fierce warriors in Afghanistan and Sindh, who moved south following Arab pressures on Sindh. Their first capital was Patdi, at the north eastern tip of Saurashtra, adjoining the Little Rann of Kutch, where they built a small castle and took over a few villages. Following successive wars with neighbouring rulers, their sovereignty extended over a much larger area of Saurashtra along the Little Rann of Kutch towards

ENTRANCE HALL OF THE RANJIT VILAS PALACE

the Arabian sea.

The arrival of the Muslim sultans in Gujarat, with their capital first at Patan and later at Ahmedabad, both too close for comfort, led to the Jhalas moving

the capital from Patdi to Halwad in the 1450s AD, following a peaceful edict issued by the Gujarat sultanate requisitioning thirty-five miles of land containing twenty-four villages very near Patdi. In the late-15th century AD, there were battles with the Gujarat sultans at Kuva and Mandal, which the Jhalas are said to have lost. According to one tale, they took back Halwad by attacking the sultan's camp at night, and forcing him at the point of a sword to give up his spoils. Another story tells us that the sultan had a Rajput wife, at whose request the capital was given back to the Jhala Rajputs, though the fortified townships of Viramgam and Mandal were retained by the Muslims under direct control. After another of these battles at Kuva, it is said, the womenfolk, assuming the battle had been lost, followed Rajput tradition and committed jauhar, which Hindu princesses and Rajput women preferred to dishonour at the hands of Muslim warriors: the armies, returning with their capital intact, found themselves widowers! But sufficient women remained for the clan to continue, and it flourished over the next 500 years. The Jhalas ruled five salute states, five non-salute states, and

RANJIT VILAS PALACE, ONE OF THE FINEST PALACES IN INDIA

numerous small jagirs at the time of Indian Independence in 1947AD, when the process of merging the princely states into the Indian Union began.

The separation of Wankaner from the elder clan at Halwad provides the backcloth for many of the romantic stories that surround the Rajput rulers of India. In the 17th century AD, goes a story, a Jhala Rajput prince of Halwad and the Mughal prince Jehangir were to marry two princesses of Jodhpur, the capital of Marwar in western Rajasthan. The question of whose wedding was to take place first was settled by a competition in horsemanship, won by the Jhala prince. But to Jehangir, who was to become the Emperor of India, this was unacceptable, and he banished the Jhalas from Halwad.

Another Jhala prince, Sartanji, came in search of a new capital to Wankaner, and set up capital in the hills. But his younger brother was instated by the Mughal emperor to the throne at Halwad, and the bitter Sartanji vowed that he would take back Halwad, or his wedding would not be a cause for celebration. In the event, he was unable to win back Halwad, and to this day the Wankaner royals have not celebrated their weddings with the pomp and glory that befit their status. Sartanji died in battle, and his wife committed sati. A beautifully carved cenotaph to the couple is located in the town.

Another distinct custom in Wankaner was that the crown prince was carefully guarded during the time of succession: this followed upon an incident in the late-18th century AD, when the rightful heir to

DRAWING ROOM OF THE RANJIT VILAS PALACE

GOTHIC ARCHWAY WITH RAJPUT JAROKHA LEADING TO THE ZANANA WING

the throne was usurped during his father's funeral. That throne was won back, but the custom was observed through subsequent generations.

By the first decade of the 19th century AD, the British had firmly established themselves in Saurashtra, and had started identifying the myriad principalities which ranged in size from a quarter of a square mile in area to huge princely states like Nawanagar (Jamnagar). Wankaner was recognised as a princely state when the Walker Settlement was signed in 1807AD. It was a second class princely

state when HH Maharajah Bane Sinhji came to the throne in 1861AD. His diwan was none other than Karamchand Gandhi, the father of arguably the world's best loved Indian freedom fighter, Mahatma Gandhi. HH Maharajah Bane Sinhji was the twelfth ruler of Wankaner's Jhala Rajput dynasty, and lived in the heart of the town, in the darbargadh, a palace in the typical Indian style with fretwork jarokha balconies, jali screens and stone carvings. When he died in 1881AD, the crown prince, Yuvraj Amar Sinhji, was only three years old, and according to the

terms of the Walker Settlement, a British resident was appointed to handle the affairs of state. Five British residents administered Wankaner from 1881AD to 1899AD, when Yuvraj Amar Sinhji was old enough to rule the state on his own.

An educated and cultured man, HH Maharajah Amar Sinhji was an excellent sportsman. He was a good cricketer in his school-days, and had won several prestigious badminton championships. He was known as a good marksman, and his love of blood sport, much glorified in those times, led him

Wankaner

to shoot a cheetah in 1901AD at Vadsar, near Wankaner, and in 1905-06AD to capture an injured cheetah alive; this was to be perhaps the last cheetah sighted in Saurashtra. He shot lions in the Gir forests in 1906AD, and went on elephant and tiger shoots in Orissa in the 1920s AD. In 1928AD, he organised a large duck shooting camp for various royal families.

Automobiles were another of HH Maharajah Amar Sinhji's passions. In 1905AD, the Maharajah of

ITALIANESQUE MARBLE FOUNTAIN AT THE RANJIT VILAS PALACE, THE CENTREPIECE OF THE FORMAL FRONT GARDENS

Bhavnagar gifted him his first car. He went on to purchase a Ford in 1910AD, a Napier a couple of years later, and a Fiat in 1914AD, which he drove to meet HH Maharajah Bhagwat Sinhji at Gondal, and even on a safari to view wild asses in Kutch. A 1921AD Rolls Royce Silver Ghost, and some imposing American cars, imported by him for the royal garages at Wankaner, are still the proud possessions of his son, HH Maharajah Pratap Sinh. In the 1920s AD, HH Maharajah Amar Sinhji graduated from cars to planes: he purchased a Handley Page in 1921AD, and by 1931AD had three aircraft. He obtained his pilot's licence in 1925AD, and introduced an airstrip for small planes in Wankaner. His wide experience of travelling overseas had included a visit to England in the summer of 1898AD with his British guardian, Hancock, and he had seen active service in France during World War II.

But it was not all fun, games and hunts for HH Maharajah Amar Sinhji. He was also a great administrator, and during his forty-nine year rule, Wankaner grew into a first class princely state with an eleven gun salute. He introduced wide-ranging reforms and public services for the betterment of the state. In the absence of major through-traffic revenues from the railways in Wankaner, agriculture was a major source of income, and the famous Wankaner milk products gave substantial support to the economy of this 425 square mile state and its

SUNSET AT THE RANJIT VILAS PALACE

101 villages. During his rule, he influenced the setting up of many industries, including a textile mill, and introduced laws to ensure that farmers were not exploited by rich landowners and merchants. The Farmers' Co-operative Bank at Wankaner was perhaps the first in Saurashtra to provide good financing facilities to the cultivators. Pension and gratuity laws were introduced for employees of the state, and a strong system of internal security made the state a peaceful place in which to live. Restrictions were imposed on tree felling. He helped start the swaraj, a self-government system advocated by Sardar Patel and Mahatma Gandhi, in the villages of Wankaner, and despite good relations with the British, gave support and shelter to the freedom fighters.

But more than anything else, HH Maharajah Amar Sinhji was a lover of architecture, and he decided that Wankaner needed a truly grand palace

DRAWING ROOM WITH VENETIAN CHANDELIER AND BALCOLNY LEADING TO THE PRINCIPAL BEDROOM OF THE RANJIT VILAS PALACE

Mughal style biradaris and Rajasthani domes. The whole ends up in a very European clock tower, surrounded by domes, kiosks and side minarets.

Behind the palace, you can see typically Rajput jarokha balconies, sometimes over a Gothic archway. An Italian marble fountain stands between the contours of the now rather dry palace lawns. The right wing of the palace is the older zanana wing, which is now used as the office of Yuvraj Dr Digvijay Sinh, the eldest son of HH Maharajah Pratap Sinh, and further to the right are the stables of Kathiawadi horses. To the left is the 1882AD residence wing, now open for house guests. A building resembling a Gothic church houses the royal garages, with horse drawn carriages, a 1921AD Rolls Royce Silver Ghost, a 1931AD Buick and other old cars, together with more modern jeeps and automobiles.

The palace's interior is as delightful as the exterior, equally impressive in its medley of styles and profusion of marble of different colours from Italy, Belgium and India, Belgian glass, crystalware from France and elsewhere in Europe, Venetian blown glass chandeliers (now, unfortunately, partially damaged), Burmese teak furniture, rugs and carpets from Persia and Mirzapur, and plush upholstered settees. A sweeping marble staircase, with Classical balustrades, takes you past Grecian urns, Rajput cusped arches, walls inlaid with Venetian and Mughal mosaics, ivory tusks and Romanesque pillars, to galleries of arched stained

in keeping with its new found status as a top-flight state. In 1907AD, he selected as the site a location halfway up a hill next to the township of Wankaner, where the British residents had already built their bungalows. The Ranjit vilas palace grounds in those days spanned 250 acres in all, climbing down from the main palace up the hill to an orchard beside the river Machchu, where he added an orchard guesthouse for Europeans and visiting royalty, called

Purna chandra bhuvan. The foundation stone for the palace was laid by HH Jam Saheb Ranjit Sinhji, the world famous cricketer and ruler of Nawanagar, after whom it is named. HH Maharajah Amar Sinhji personally oversaw the design of the palace, with a bold synthesis of styles. Victorian arcades lead to a facade in the Venetian-Gothic manner, with pointed Gothic arches and Italianesque pillars. The roof is rather in the Dutch tradition, and above it are two

Wankaner

ENTRANCE TO THE RANJIT VILAS PALACE

DINING ROOM OF THE RANJIT VILAS PALACE

glass windows. One of the windows bears the signature of HH Maharajah Amar Sinhji, while others have the Wankaner crest.

The drawing room, behind the base of the staircase, has beautiful sofas and other furnishings. A throne in the form of a silver lion, made for the then crown prince, HH Maharajah Pratap Sinh, who now owns the palace and who has recently celebrated his 91st birthday, stands in a corner of the drawing room. Huge Venetian chandeliers, and a selection

from the eighty-five species of stuffed animals, shot by the royal family during trips round the world, have been mounted on the walls. On the right of the drawing room as you enter is the banqueting hall, with an elegant wooden dining table, glass cabinets with a collection of crockery and silverware, some more hunting trophies, an intricately decorated ceiling and arches ranging in style from Moorish to Venetian-Gothic. On the upper storeys of the palace are the family's apartments. The old suite of HH

Maharajah Amar Sinhji has been retained in its original state, with Art Deco furniture, a beautiful rolltop desk and fine portraits. From here, a secret spiral staircase leads one way to the old darbargadh, which is still used as the court of law, and, to the other, down to the cellar, where the family's treasures are kept.

Another room displays a beautiful silver elephant howdah and fabulous caparisons for elephants and horses. Another room has standards, insignia and the

STEPPED WELL IN TYPICAL RAJPUT AND EUROPEAN STYLES AT THE RANJIT VILAS PALACE

(TOP) **SIDE VIEW OF THE RANJIT VILAS PALACE**
(BOTTOM) **ENTRANCE HALL WITH SWEEPING MARBLE STAIRCASE AT THE RANJIT VILAS PALACE**

Wankaner

GROUND FLOOR ENTRANCE TO THE STEPPED WELL AT THE RANJIT VILAS PALACE

The devotional aspects of the Rajputs are visible in beautiful miniature temples and swings for Lord Krishna.

Much of the 250 acres of land now belongs to private residences, temples, public offices and potteries, which separate the palace from the thirty-three acre royal orchard, where the Purna chandra bhuvan offers rooms furnished in the Art Deco style, some with Art Deco style baths en suite, together with an Art Deco style indoor swimming pool, and a forecourt with fountains and pools. A stepped well with three storeys, two of which are below ground, offers Classical balustraded marble steps leading down to cool chambers for relaxing. A fountain in the centre of the well acts as a natural air conditioning system. Given the Hindu love for decoration, it is not surprising that the stepwell is embellished with intricate Hindu devotional marble sculpture.

HH Maharajah Amar Sinhji did not confine his architectural obsession to Wankaner alone, however. He built the palatial Wankaner mansion in Bombay, which is now the Consulate of the United States of America, and the Amar Building, also in Bombay, now the Reserve Bank of India.

HH Maharajah Pratap Sinh shares his father's love for automobiles, and has an impressive number of books on cars. A graduate of Cambridge University, he was an active politician. Yuvraj Dr Digvijay Sinh, who also went to Cambridge, is a

coat of arms. Shields, spears and a memorable collection of swords and daggers, dating from those given to the early rulers of Wankaner to those received during recent Delhi darbars, hold pride of place in the old armoury, alongside a number of pistols and other guns for duelling and hunting, and spears for pigsticking. Nearby, sport enthusiasts can look forward to seeing shotguns, rifles, golf clubs, skis and other sports equipment of a kind not easily available today. In another part of the cellar, a beautiful maharajah's throne from Banares is flanked by thrones for the princes and relatives. Among the works of art seen here is a fabulous painting from Nathdwara, near Udaipur, and local handcrafts include textiles, silver and the kind of chests called pataras and majoos peculiar to Kathiawad.

ART DECO SWIMMING POOL WITH HAMMER BEAM STYLE ROOF AT THE RANJIT VILAS PALACE

UPPER FLOOR GALLERY IN MARBLE WITH TILED FLOORING AT THE RANJIT VILAS PALACE

riding enthusiast, usually seen in breeches, and is among those people working hard to conserve the Kathiawadi horses typical of this region. An active politician like his father, he often represented Wankaner as a member of Parliament, and is a one-time Union cabinet minister for the environment. He is now convenor of the Gujarat chapter of the Heritage Hotels Association, and is working to develop the properties of Wankaner, among the first in India to take tourists as the guests of royal families, into the more professionally managed system of Heritage Hotels. One of his current projects is the introduction of land sailing as a sport in the Little Rann of Kutch, where the flat terrain and keen winds combine to offer considerable potential for this sport. He has also written a book on ecology.

His younger brother, Yuvraj Ranjit Sinh, is a wildlife enthusiast, actually a hunter turned conservationist, who has often served in an honourable capacity on the Indian Board of Wildlife, and is the author of 'Blackbuck', a book on the Indian antelope of the same name. Together, the two brothers are working to convert the royal grasslands, which were once harvested for the princely state's cattle and provided the family with game, into a nature reserve.

Other States and Areas of Gujarat

Idar

Idar was one of the most prominent princely states in the whole of Gujarat. The fort of Idar stood between Rajasthan and the fertile lands of Gujarat, and invaders had to take on Idar before moving into Gujarat. The fort, therefore, witnessed many great sieges, battles and skirmishes. Today, the royal family lives in its palace at Himmatnagar and in apartments in Bombay. The family has a stud farm and breeds thoroughbred horses for racing.

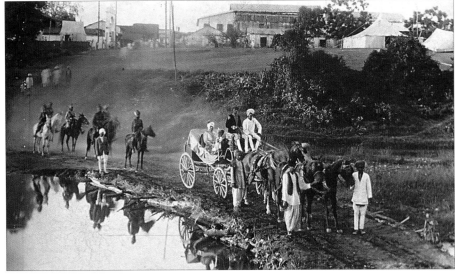

ROYAL CARRIAGE PROCESSION ALONG THE LAKESIDE

Cambay

Cambay was another important state, and had a port of considerable importance, before this was silted up by the dangerously strong tides of the Gulf of Cambay. The Shiya Muslim dynasty set up state at Cambay.

There are some fine palaces at Santrampur, Lunawada and Devgadh Baria, but these we have not covered, as the owners have no plans to open them to tourists.

British Provinces in Gujarat

The British exercised direct control over certain regions within Gujarat, and some of their old buildings still remain.

Ahmedabad was the historic Karnawati or Ashawal, rated among the beautiful cities of 11th century AD India. After a period of oblivion, the city regained importance when Sultan Ahmed Shah decided to move his capital from Patan to a new city founded on the banks of the river Sabarmati. This was named Ahmedabad, as the foundation stone in 1411AD was laid by four Ahmeds: by Sultan Ahmed Shah; by Shaik Ahmed Ganj Baksh, a man revered by the sultans at Sarkhej near Ahmedabad; by Ahmed Malek and by Ahmed Kaji. By 1414AD the new capital was ready. The city gained in stature under the sultans, and was endowed with some 200 mosques, many of which survive; with medieval walls having numerous bastions and towers; with a fort palace, stepwells, a dozen intricate carved gates and with exquisite royal mausolea. The Arabian historian, Udadbir, the Spanish traveller, Baroboza, and other visitors are said to have been impressed by the scale of the city. In 1572AD, Emperor Akhbar captured Ahmedabad and annexed it to his formidable Mughal empire.

Political relations with the British began in 1617AD when Sir Thomas Roe visited Ahmedabad and described it in *The Embassy of Sir Thomas Roe to India* as "a goodly city, large as London". The Mughal emperor Jehangir visited Ahmedabad during Sir Thomas Roe's stay in the city, and wrote a letter for the English king James I, establishing political and trade relationships. Following upon the appointment of the emperor's son, Shah Jahan, as subhedar of Ahmedabad, the Shahibagh palace was commissioned and the Shahi gardens laid in 1621AD. After Shah Jahan succeeded Jehangir as Emperor of India in 1627AD, the Badhra palace was constructed in Ahmedabad for the subhedar, Azam Khan. Aurangzeb seized the Mughal empire from his father, Shah Jahan, in 1658AD; new relations were forged with European nations, and concessions given to European businessmen, who began to set up export trade centres in Gujarat.

The Marathas rose as the major power upon the ruins of the Mughal empire, and the Gaekwads took over Ahmedabad in the late-17th century AD. In 1818AD, Gaekwadi rule was ended in Ahmedabad, and the British took direct control, with Mr Dunlop, the collector of Kaira, as the representative. European imports began in 1820AD and a number

of colonial buildings in Venetian-Gothic and Renaissance styles were constructed in the city in the 19th century AD. The 1864AD railway link between Ahmedabad and Bombay heralded the birth of the golden corridor of industry in western India. The British had limited importance in Ahmedabad in the late-19th and early-20th centuries AD, as the local population was enterprising, and textile mills, libraries, schools and colleges were introduced by benevolent citizens, and funded by business communities. Freedom fighters, under leaders like Mahatma Gandhi and Sardar Vallabhbhai Patel, fought for the introduction of local self-government.

Kaira, or Kheda, was an important British stronghold under the collectorate. The town still has old towers, schools, police stations and offices built during the colonial period. Important bridges, over rivers like the Mahi, were commissioned by the collector to connect Ahmedabad with Bombay.

Surat was the most important British province in Gujarat. Surat had been an important port during the sultanate and Mughal periods; it had seen considerable Portuguese influence in the 16th century AD, Dutch trade posts were set up in Surat from 1620AD, the French arrived there in 1644AD, and the Portuguese and Persians also had factories there. But it was the British who brought prosperity to Surat. In 1608AD, Emperor Jehangir issued an edict enabling the British to establish industry in Surat. By 1612AD, the first British factory had been

ROYAL WEDDING PROCESSION

inaugurated. From then on, the British, with a series of opportune treaties, changing alliances and far-sighted policies, presided over the growth of Surat, which became a major British stronghold. The British factories were like integral villages, with strong stone walls and wood carvings, presidential rooms, gardens, palm groves and residences, often near the rivers. A British cemetery, Dutch tombs and other European graveyards sprang up in Surat.

After the British took control of Gujarat, nawabs were appointed to govern Surat in the 18th century AD. Though the Mahida Rajputs ruled Mandvi, near Surat, they were little more than puppets of the British, and by the late-19th century AD, the region had been taken directly under British rule. The English High School was inaugurated in 1872AD, and the Andrews public library, named after a retired magistrate, in 1907AD; and the Victoria garden, the 1824AD Christ Church, the 1874AD Hope Bridge, named after the British collector, and the English wharf are other reminders of British rule in Surat.

PORTUGUESE FORT AT DIU

PORTRAIT OF A YOUNG PRINCE

Portuguese Enclaves

The Portuguese controlled much of India's sea trade, especially on the west coast, and retained control of Goa, Daman and the island of Diu, the last two in Gujarat, even after the British left India.

Diu was an important harbour for the Chudasama Rajputs of Junagadh in the 13th century AD, and was taken by the Muslim sultans. By the 15th century AD, it was a significant port controlling trade between the middle east and far east, and a shipbuilding centre. The Sultan of Gujarat ruled Diu with the support of the powerful Ottoman army. Malek Ayaz, a subhedar of Saurashtra appointed by the sultan, administered the port. He repelled Portuguese invaders in the 1520s AD. After his death, the Portuguese teamed up with his son, Ishak, and took over Diu, but were overwhelmed by Ishak's younger brother, Tughan, who recaptured Diu for the sultanate with the support of his Ottoman allies, Amir Mustafa and Khwaja Safar. But the Portuguese considered Diu important enough to murder for, and, inviting Sultan Bahadur Shah on board a ship to sign a treaty, had him killed treacherously. The Portuguese became lords of Diu in the 1530s AD. Sulaiman Pasha, Greek governor of Egypt, attacked Diu with his Ottoman armies, but could not take the formidable coastal fort under Nuno da Cunha. Khwaja Safar's attack on Diu in 1546AD was routed.

With Diu under their control, the Portuguese became masters of the Saurashtra sea coast; no vessel could enter, or leave, its waters without Portuguese consent, and this was given only at a certain price, or the vessel would need to take on the mighty ships built in Diu. The British and the Dutch found that piracy was the only way to undermine Portuguese domination in western India.

Diu's fort is perhaps the largest on India's west coast, encircled by a wall over five kilometres long. Impressive gateways mark the entrance. The ramparts are guarded by cannon and the bastions named after Christian saints. Inside the fort, you find a cathedral, a subhedar's palace, barracks, watchtowers and dwellings. The sea all but surrounds the fort, and two moats, one tidal, protect the landlocked side of the fort.

Catholic churches with superb Baroque and Gothic style facades proliferated during Portuguese rule of the island. Services are still held at St Paul's Church. St Thomas' Church is now a museum of figurines and statues of Christian saints, of Christ and of the Virgin Mary, while St Francis' Church is a primary health centre. Other Portuguese buildings are now schools and offices. It is said that the Portuguese blew up some important buildings when the Indian navy took over the island in 1961AD.

Daman, like Diu, was an important sea trade post for centuries – in fact it has an even longer history. The Mauryan emperors up to the 4th century AD,

CHAPEL, DIU FORT

TYPICAL PORTUGUESE COLONIAL ARCHITECTURE, DIU

the Kshatrapas who succeeded them as rulers, the Solanki Rajputs in the 11th century AD and the Rajput chieftain, Ramashah, in 1293AD: all had realised the potential of Daman. The Portuguese settled in Goa from 1510AD, took Daman without serious opposition in 1531AD, but had subsequently to deal with the Sultan of Gujarat. An agreement was drawn up, and the customs revenues shared. An Abyssinian governor, appointed by the sultan to represent the sultanate in dealings with the Portuguese, revolted. The Portuguese under Dom Constantino de Braganca launched a strong onslaught in 1558-59AD, with one hundred ships manned by 3,000 men, and took Daman without, it is said, losing a single life. Dom Diogo de Noronha was declared commander of Daman. There are numerous forts, churches, cathedrals, cemeteries and war memorials built by the Portuguese in Daman. Mass is still held, and Christmas celebrated in the churches.

When the Indian navy took over Diu and Daman, Portuguese rule in India ended. Interestingly enough, it was the Portuguese who remained the longest colonial rulers of India: their rule, of some 400 years, compares comfortably with the Mughal dynasty, of some 200 years, and with the British rule, similarly of about 200 years!

ROYAL CELEBRATIONS

Travel to Gujarat

BALARAM PALACE, PALANPUR

TRAVEL TO AND AROUND GUJARAT

Air India and other airlines operate flights to Ahmedabad from London, New York and countries in the Middle East and South East Asia. More frequent flights connect Bombay, Delhi, Calcutta and Madras to Ahmedabad, convenient for those who have specific airline preferences. There are domestic flights from Bombay to Baroda, Bhavnagar, Rajkot, Porbandar, Jamnagar, Keshod near Junagadh and Bhuj-Kutch. Trains offer a comfortable and economical way to travel from Bombay or Delhi to destinations in Gujarat, and within the state. Most trains have first class air conditioned compartments, second class air conditioned sleeper cars and first class non-air conditioned compartments, each of them with shared bathroom (English style toilets) down the corridor. Second class should be avoided unless you are on a really tight budget, or are of the adventurous kind, looking to experience travel with the locals. State transport buses (ST buses) are meant for short distance local travel, and are avoidable, but privately run coaches with reclining seats can offer a cheap and not too uncomfortable way to journey between destinations. The best way to tour the state is to hire a chauffeur driven car for your journey. Cities like Ahmedabad can offer a wide range of air conditioned and non-air conditioned cars, mini-buses and coaches. Diesel cars are considerably cheaper than petrol ones. Few drivers speak much English, but most can understand what you are saying. Tour operators usually offer you a good choice of itineraries and vehicles.

TRAVEL AGENTS AND TOUR OPERATORS

It is not easy for tourists to travel alone in Gujarat, as tourism in the state is still in its infancy. Package tours featuring the Heritage Hotels of Gujarat are offered by Cox & Kings Travel Ltd, by Pettitts India of Tunbridge Wells, by Eastravel Ltd of Ipswich, by Indus Tours and Travel Ltd of Harrow, by Andrew Brock Travel Ltd of Uppingham, and by Hampstead Heath Travel, Trans Indus Ltd and Western & Oriental Travel Ltd of London. The author travelled through a small, but efficient, travel operator, North West Safaris, 91/92 Kamdhenu Complex, Ambawadi, Ahmedabad-380015, Gujarat, telephone: 0091-79-6442019/ 408031/6441511, or fax: 0091-79-6560962. Their arrangements, by theme, include *'royal holidays'*, with accommodation in various palaces and other Heritage Hotels and meetings with royal families; *'textile and handcraft tours'*, featuring private collections of textiles and handcrafts in palaces and artisans' workshops in villages, towns and bazaars; *'battlefield history and military architecture tours'*, featuring historic forts, palaces and battlefields; *'art, architecture and art history tours'*, featuring private art collections and monuments; *'historic architecture and archaelogical tours'*, taking in various sites of historic importance; and *'wildlife and nature tours'*, which blend visits to wildlife sanctuaries and national parks with stays in palaces and castles facing lakes, rivers and wildlife areas.

LANGUAGE

The principal language of Gujarat is Gujarati, spoken with many dialects, the kind spoken in the Kathiawadi peninsula being quite different from that of the cities in the north and south of India. Hindi is widely spoken. Almost every town or city has an English medium school, and so English is spoken sufficiently for a person to get by, and you are almost certain to find someone who speaks English at bus stations, post offices, restaurants and hotels; and milestones and sign boards in English are also very common.

CHANGING MONEY

The Indian currency is based on the decimal system, with 100 paise amounting to one rupee. At the time of the author's visit, the exchange rates were Rs.58 to £1 sterling, or Rs.39 to US$1. The best place to change money is in Ahmedabad, where there are a good number of licenced money changing firms – which are quicker than the government nationalised banks and are open for longer hours – besides many private banks. £ sterling and US$ are usually preferred to other currencies. Travellers' cheques of Thomas Cook, American Express and other banks are welcomed – you may well get better rates for travellers' cheques than for currency at some banks. A few banks will advance money against credit cards like VISA. Banks will also change money in Baroda, Bhavnagar, Junagadh, Gondal, Rajkot, Jamnagar, Porbandar and Bhuj-Kutch.

ACCOMMODATION AND ACCESS

Taking a leaf out of the book of the Palace Hotels in Rajasthan, many former royal families have converted their properties into Heritage Hotels, or leased them to hotel chains and private entrepreneurs. Numerous palaces and forts were taken over by the government after Independence, or purchased by government departments for various purposes. These properties are now museums, archeological monuments, schools, universities, colleges, government offices or collectorates. Some properties have been sold, rented or donated to religious and social trusts for their offices. However, a number of palaces are still the private residences of the royal families, and visits can be arranged only by prior appointment.

It is a good idea to ask before taking photographs, and barging into a palace is just not done. Royal families are usually friendly and hospitable, and you will find yourself quite welcome, once you contact them for permission.

Ahmedabad

Ahmedabad has a wide choice of hotels and restaurants, but no Heritage Hotel. The **Shahibagh palace** of the Mughal dynasty is now the **Sardar Patel museum**; the **Sarkhej palace** is an archeological museum; and the **Badhra fort palace** is probably the world's prettiest post office.

Balasinore

The **Garden palace** of Balasinore, 86 kilometres

ORCHARD PALACE, GONDAL

from Ahmedabad, is now an Heritage Hotel, run by the royal family of Balasinore in the house guest tradition. Guests can chat with the family in the beautiful French furnished drawing room, enjoy authentic Mughali cuisine in the dining hall, and stay in any of the four rooms appointed with a combination of old and new furniture, works of art and modern bathrooms. The Garden palace has its own orchards, fields, poultry and dairy, and the meals are made from home-grown fruit and vegetables. The royal family proposes to open more rooms in the Lake house and European guesthouse. By night, guests can be entertained by tribal dancers, and by day may travel by jeep safari to the dinosaur site, where 65 million year-old dinosaur fossils and eggs have been excavated, or by taxi tour to the semi-sulphuric hot water springs at Lasundra, and the numerous historic temples nearby.

Baroda

Baroda has at present only one Heritage Hotel, the **Chandod palace**. The **Sarita Heritage Hotel**, a 19th century AD haveli, with simple homecooked

Travel

food, fifty-five kilometres from Baroda, and forty kilometres from Rajpipla, is worth a visit.

The **Laxmi vilas palace** of Baroda is not an Heritage Hotel, and is inaccessible to visitors, but great views of the palace can be enjoyed from the road and nearby buildings. A selection of art treasures from the palace, including portraits, copies of European masters, original European paintings, bronzes, marble statues, Chinese and Japanese art, chandeliers and carvings are exhibited at the **Maharajah Fateh Sinhji museum** in the complex, and there is an entry fee of Rs.10/adult and Rs.5/child. The Motibagh grounds in the palace have sports facilities, including golf and cricket. The **Pratap vilas palace** at Lalbagh is now the Railway Staff College, and you can enjoy splendid views of the domes and facade from the neatly landscaped gardens. The **Shiv mahal palace** is being restored, and may be converted into an hotel very soon. The **Kirti mandir** royal monument is open to visitors. The **Baroda museum**, built for the purpose in the late-19th century AD, has galleries of portraits and royal memorabilia.

Bhavnagar

The **Nilambagh palace** of Bhavnagar is now an Heritage Hotel with a beautiful lobby, a grand dining hall, air conditioned rooms with TV, telephone and bathrooms en suite; a travel information desk, moneychanging counter, multi-cuisine restaurant, garden restaurant, lawns, swimming pool, tennis courts, conference hall,

library and other facilities. The old darbargadh, complete with arches and carved balconies, is now the State Bank office. There is also a second Heritage Hotel, the **Palace Utelia Hotel**. The **Bhav vilas palace** is still a private residence, and permission is required for a visit. The **Dil bahar palace**, with four guest rooms, a swimming pool and a great quantity of memorabilia, occasionally takes paying house guests.

Chotta Udaipur

The **Kusum vilas palace** of Chotta Udaipur is being restored, and there are plans to convert it into an Heritage Hotel very soon. Other palaces in Chotta Udaipur house government offices, schools and hostels.

Gondal

Gondal has two Heritage Hotels, run by the royal family: the **Orchard palace**, a wing of their own **Huzoor palace**, and the **Riverside palace**, one kilometre away. They offer good Indian and continental food, and guests have access to the **Naulakha palace** and the vintage and classic car garages, and may be invited for a meal in the French furnished drawing room at the Huzoor palace.

Jamnagar

Jamnagar has a number of city hotels for corporates and businessmen, but no Heritage Hotel or scenic resorts. The **Lakota palace** is now a museum, and can be visited.

Jasdan

The **Hingolgadh castle** of the royal family of Jasdan is now an Heritage Hotel, and welcomes guests as

part of the family. The castle has pleasantly old-fashioned rooms with bathrooms en suite and toilets, and offers continental meals. It is in the heart of a sanctuary; and gazelle, antelope, jackal and jungle cat can be seen from the castle itself. Guests can ask the owners for access to their palace and stud farm. The family takes guests as if they are part of a house party.

Junagadh

Junagadh has a few budget hotels, basically for Indian salesmen, some with air conditioned rooms, but it is just one hour from Gondal, and the hotels can be used as a base for excursions to Junagadh and Gondal.

Kutch

Kutch has the **Aina mahal palace, Pragmahal palace** and **Sharad bagh palace** in Bhuj, and the **Vijay palace** at Mandvi, and all four are now Heritage Hotels. There are also some fairly good hotels in Bhuj, and in nearby Gandhidham, cottages by the sea at Mandvi, and pleasant country resorts like the **GL Sharma resort** on the Bhuj-Gandhidham road.

Limbdi

Limbdi is starting a resort and already has a motel. Those staying here can ask permission to see the **Digbhuvan**.

Palanpur

Palanpur's **Zoravar palace** is now a court of law, and can be visited, though photography of the interior is strictly prohibited. The **Balaram palace**, an Heritage Hotel, fifteen minutes from Palanpur, is now a resort blending 1920s AD and 1930s AD architecture with modern amenities like a swimming pool, gym, multi-cuisine restaurant, air conditioned rooms with refrigerator, TV, telephone, and modern bathrooms. It accepts credit cards, and has facilities for money-changing, cycle hire and car rental. The **Poshina darbargadh**, a small fort in the heart of a colourful tribal area, and a half-hour drive from Palanpur, is now a family-run Heritage Hotel. A must for those wanting to experience royal hospitality, medieval ambience and life among the hill tribes.

Porbandar

Porbandar has some reasonably good hotels in the city and near the sea. The **Daria rajmahal** is now a college, and can be visited. The **Huzoor palace** requires permission from the office to see the interior.

Rajkot

Rajkot has city hotels for business travellers, but there are plans to open one of the royal properties as an Heritage Hotel. In the meantime, you can make the trip from either of the Heritage Hotels at Gondal, a forty-five minute drive, or Wankaner, an one-hour drive. The **Ranjit vilas palace** is not yet open for visitors, but meanwhile you can see some princely memorabilia at the **Watson museum.**

Rajpipla

The **Vijay palace** in Rajpipla has been converted into the **Vijayraj palace hotel**, an Heritage Hotel, and its annexe is the **Rajwant resort**. The palace offers period furnishings and modern facilities,

PALIAS, KUTCH

including a swimming pool, multi-cuisine restaurant, air conditioning and indoor games, and a museum of princely effects. There are plans for a tribal museum and cultural centre within the palace grounds. The **Kirti bhuvan**, a royal mansion, is now a guesthouse for business visitors to Rajpipla. The **Natwar niwas palace** may be opened as an Heritage Hotel in due course.

Wadhwan

Wadhwan's **Rajmahal** is being renovated with a view to it becoming an Heritage Hotel.

Wankaner

Wankaner has two Heritage Hotels – the **Royal Oasis hotel**, once the **Purna chandra bhuvan**, and the **Residency hotel**, once the **Khengar bhuvan**, both erstwhile guesthouses. Guests of both hotels may be invited for meals to the **Ranjit vilas palace**, and can ask to see the museum.

SAFETY FACTORS

Physical assault and mugging incidents are almost unknown in Gujarat, but the possibility of petty theft should never be ruled out. For this reason, do not leave valuables in hotel rooms – most hotels have their own safe-deposit lockers – and do not keep expensive items like cameras and binoculars near car or room windows unattended. Watch out for pick-pockets in crowded areas like railway booking queues and bus stations. Waist pouches and hidden pockets are better places than hip pockets in which to keep money. Women are very safe in Gujarat, even unaccompanied, but they should avoid wearing revealing, or apparently outlandish, clothes. Shorts and miniskirts should also be avoided during journeys, and while walking in the street.

Staring is not considered rude in India, as it would be in the west, and the people of Gujarat tend to be very inquisitive. Indeed, it would be considered as rude not to be curious and inquisitive in Gujarat, as it would be to stare at people in the west! The author once witnessed a villager asking an English woman at a lake in Gujarat if he might borrow her binoculars, and, taking her nod for a yes, tried to take them from her, which she interpreted as harassment or grabbing. While visiting a fort, the author met a tribal woman who took pride in her ancestors' association with the fort's history, and showed people around the monument without expecting any money, giving any proceeds from tips to the temple in the fort – only to be told by some European travellers that she was showing people around for baksheesh! Such misunderstandings between the locals and tourists are not uncommon in India.

PASSPORTS AND VISAS

For up-to-date information, contact the Indian High Commission in your country.

FOOD, WATER AND CUISINE

Gujarati food is predominantly vegetarian, and is fairly kind to the stomach if you ask them to go easy on the chillies and oil. Most northern Gujarati dishes are sweetened with jaggery or sugar, the Kathiawadi dishes have more chillies and garlic, and Kutchi food has Sindhi influences.

Gujarati thalis are quick, cheap and wholesome, with potato curry, two green vegetables, beans or chickpeas, rotis made from millet and wheat, fresh country butter, steamed rice, kadi and local sweet delicacies: a complete mix of nutrients, in fact!

North Indian (Punjabi and Mughali) food is richer and more varied, with chicken, mutton (goat/lamb meat), fish, paneer, mushrooms, green vegetables, cabbages, cauliflowers etc, cooked in rich tomato curries laced with homemade butter, local cheeses and even nuts and dried fruits, with a variety of rotis, naans, biryanis or pulaos. Tandoori dishes like paneer tikka, chicken tikka, tandoori chicken, tandoori fish etc, barbecued in clay ovens and

marinaded with spices, are the firm favourites of most travellers to India. If the word masala is added to the tandoori item, eg. chicken tikka masala, it usually means it comes with a spicy gravy. Continental food is available in large cities like Ahmedabad, Baroda, Bhavnagar, Jamnagar, Rajkot, Bhuj and Junagadh. Heritage Hotels offer continental food and subtly spiced Indian food, designed for tourists from the west.

Buffets in large hotels usually have soup, salad, and Indian, Chinese and western counters. At some restaurants in Rajkot or Jamnagar, baked dishes may be sweetened with sugar in a white sauce or chunks of pineapple – check before you order! As elsewhere in the world, Chinese food has its own local version in India, adapted to Indian tastes. Good fast food restaurants, hotel coffee shops and cafes in Ahmedabad and Baroda offer pizzas, burgers, fried fish etc of a reasonably good standard, but in smaller places you usually get the local version – pizza could be a spicy tomato ketchup sauce, chopped onions and unmelted grated processed cheese on a crisp toast. Street food stalls and hand-carts offer cheap and good food, but are not very hygienic; if you have to eat there while waiting for a train or a bus, stick to food prepared hot in front of you.

Water used to be a major hazard in India, and though now most affluent houses, hotels and good restaurants have water purifiers which boil and filter the water, it is safer to stick to bottled mineral water,

KIRTI MANDIR, THE MEMORIAL TO MAHATMA GANDHI, PORBANDAR

aerated soft drinks and well boiled tea, coffee or milk. Water at public places, like railway stations, should be avoided altogether. For the same reason, one should avoid exposed fruit and uncooked vegetables, because one can never be quite sure whether – or where – they have been washed. Mutton and chicken should only be eaten at reputable hotels and restaurants, where they are properly washed and boiled.

Gujarat offers some of India's best ice-creams. Vadilal is the most popular ice-cream brand. Havmour is good, too. Baskin Robbins has also introduced its ice-cream in Gujarat. Different areas have particular brands – Dilbahar is a popular ice-cream in Bhavnagar, as are Patel and Rajasthan ice-creams in

Ahmedabad, and Pestonjee in southern Gujarat.

Sundaes are available at Vadilal and Havmour parlours. Soft ice-cream parlours make western style ice-cream on imported European machines. Kulfis are Indian ice-creams, rich and creamy, with lots of nuts.

Tea in Gujarat is usually strong and milky, flavoured with mint, cardamom, ginger or cinnamon, and comes as a ready-made mixture. If you do not care for Indian tea, ask for service tea at hotels – this refers to the self-service system of English tea – or carry your own tea bags, and order hot water and milk.

Gujarat has excellent sweet delicacies, with Rajkot and Bhavnagar being especially well known. There are a number of snacks like chaklis, chevdas etc, which go well with tea. Fresh bread, butter, milk and eggs are available in all cities and towns, if you want to make picnics of some of your meals.

HEALTH

Vaccinations to be taken etc: refer to your doctor.

TOILETS AND BATHING FACILITIES

Rooms in Heritage Hotels and other good hotels have bathrooms en suite, with English style toilets and hot and cold showers and taps. Often, you may find geysers, which have to be switched on (a red light comes on, indicating that the water is being heated), instead of central hot water systems. If you

ENTRANCE TO THE DARBARHALL MUSEUM, JUNAGADH

cannot find the hot water switch, ask the hotel management. In bathrooms with geysers, sinks may not have hot water – if you need hot water for shaving etc, take it from the bath taps or showers. In cheaper hotels, and instead of showers, you may find taps from which you have to fill buckets for your bath. Cheap guesthouses provide hot water in buckets. Towels, soap and toilet tissue are changed daily in hotels used to tourists, but in some smaller hotels, you may not find toilet tissue – so carry a set with you.

HOSPITALITY

Hospitality in Gujarat can be overwhelming, and people very helpful and friendly. Even at buffets and thalis, where fixed amounts are charged, you will find the staff and management offering you lots of refills, and almost forcing you to try new things and take more helpings. When visiting people, including complete strangers, you are certain to be offered tea, coffee and soft drinks with generous helpings of snacks, and even invited for a meal. Poor villagers and tribals will not hesitate to offer you a cup of tea, and a spoonful of whatever they are eating. Travellers from the west are often surprised that people will go out of their way to help them, and to ensure they are comfortable. You may find people too pushy or forceful in offering food, but this is part of Gujarati custom. The driver of your taxi may willingly take locals to their place of work when he knows you do not need the car, but this generally has nothing to do with getting money or tips – it is just part of a friendly tradition.

CONDUCT

Indians look askance at unmarried couples taking a room, homosexuality, women smoking or drinking, grown men in shorts or women wearing bikinis, miniskirts, shorts or backless dresses. The more formally you dress, the more highly people will rate you, and even hotel staff have scant respect for tourists in shorts and T-shirts, whom they look upon as backpackers. Shaking hands with members of the opposite sex is not normal in India. Indian women, outside westernised circles, tend to be shy and modest, and seldom like to be photographed. At religious places, whether at temples, mosques, or gurudwaras, cover yourself well from head to ankle.

TIPPING

It is customary to tip Rs.5 per piece of luggage at hotels, 10% of the bill in restaurants, and around 5% of the car rental bill to your driver. Porterage at certain stations and airports, where it is not already stipulated by regulations, is best negotiated in advance.

WHEN TO VISIT

Gujarat is most pleasant in winter from late-October to very early-March, when nights are cool, and days are reasonably warm. April to June should be avoided, when it can get really hot, except if you restrict your stay to hotels with air conditioned or air-cooled rooms, travel by an air conditioned car and do your sightseeing only early-mornings and late-evenings, as the author did on his first research trip to Gujarat. The south west monsoon, from July to September, is pleasant and beautiful, but makes visiting some of the forts and rural castles difficult, and sometimes the days can become humid.

WHAT TO CARRY

A blend of warm woollens and cool cottons are recommended for winter visitors. Do not let the temperatures fool you: 5 degrees centigrade may seem like a warm summer night in some parts of Europe, but the strong winds blowing across the plains of Kathiawad and the Kutch desert can make the toughest tourist shiver, if not properly covered. Carry a set of toilet and other tissues. Air-cushions and pillows can make travel easier on rough roads. A sleeping bag, or extra sheets and a foam mattress, can be useful if you are planning to stay in cheaper hotels. While carrying electrical or rechargeable battery operated appliances, remember that the voltage in India is 210/220, and that a suitable travel adaptor should be taken with you

PHOTOGRAPHY

Carry plenty of film, and if you need to replenish stock, do it in the major cities. Development of negatives and slides is of a fairly good standard in Ahmedabad, and 'manual enlargements', referring to hand-done or hand-finished enlarging, is well recommended. Many laboratories will have your film ready in a few hours, or certainly by the next day, and this is recommended if you are trying any experimental photography, or want to give photographs as gifts to your hosts. It is often a good idea to ask before taking photographs of buildings, or of people. Video camera fees for some monuments and sanctuaries can be quite steep.

SHOPPING

Gujarat has a wealth of ethnic handcrafts which are well worth shopping for during your visit. What you buy depends mainly on whether you are seeking souvenirs, curios or things for everyday use.

Textiles are a good buy in Gujarat. Gujarat is famous for rich embroideries, often supplemented by mirror inlays or appliqué-work, and these are available everywhere, with Kutch offering the brightest colours and patterns. You can purchase ready-to-wear or semi-stitched Indian dresses, fabrics, bed covers and wall hangings; or useful articles like purses, wall hangings with pockets for stationery and letters, and cloth bound files. Block and screen printing of textiles is another Gujarati craft, and you can buy bed linen, sarees and Indian and western dresses. Tie-dyed textiles, called bandhini, are almost synonymous with Gujarat, with Jamnagar, Kutch and Ahmedabad being considered the best places to buy tie-dyed scarves, sarees, shawls and dresses. Pitloom woven rugs can be bought in Kutch, handloom woven textiles anywhere in Gujarat, and beadwork wall hangings in Gondal.

Gujarat is famous for its silver ornaments, and you can pick up earrings, noserings and bangles of a good standard in Kutch, Rajkot, Gondal, Wadhwan and Wankaner, and chunky tribal silver jewellery in Kutch, Chotta Udaipur and the villages near Palanpur and Poshina. Brass objects can be bought at Jamnagar, Gondal and Jasdan. Jewellery made

GATEWAY TO THE CITY PALACE, PORBANDAR

from semi-precious stones like agate or jasper is a major industry along the Gulf of Cambay. Morvi and Wankaner are known for their pottery and ceramics. Tribal pottery and terracotta figures of horses and elephants can be purchased in Poshina in northern Gujarat and Chotta Udaipur. Wood carving is a major craft in Kutch. Lacquered wood furniture and utensils are made in Sankheda, near Baroda. Curios and antiques can be bought at Dhoraji, near Gondal, and at Surendranagar, near Wadhwan. Embroidered leather goods are made in Kutch and Radhanpur.

There is much more besides handcrafts that can be bought in Gujarat. Cotton shirts, gowns and dresses are much cheaper than in Europe. The scrap

auctioned by the ship-breaking yards of Alang, near Bhavnagar, include beautiful furniture, electronic goods, pianos and other products in good condition salvaged from ships, and are available at a fraction of the price you might pay in the west. Some travellers find Gujarat a good place to buy jewellery, due to the lower rates for cutting and polishing precious stones. English books can be bought in India at far lower prices than you might pay in Europe or America. Labour here is skilled and cheap, and can make custom-made products to order at reasonable prices.

Hotels often have counters or shopping arcades where such handcrafts can be bought as gifts. If you are a keen shopper or collector, do explore the local markets. Each city or town has one major marketplace, with lanes called bazaars dedicated to different products.

COMMUNICATIONS

PCOs (public call offices) are prolific in Gujarat, and you will find them in every city and town, as well as on the highways at regular intervals. STD refers to out-station calls within India, and ISD to international calls. The charges are around Rs.2/minute over and above the actual cost of the phone call. Many PCOs have fax facilities at Rs.10/A4 size page over and above the actual cost of the call, and will take your replies at Rs.10/A4 size page. E-mail and internet is becoming quite common in large cities like Ahmedabad, Baroda,

Bhavnagar and Rajkot. The author communicated by e-mail through Log-in, 92 Kamdhenu Complex, Ambawadi, Ahmedabad, and messages reached England within a few hours. Internet cafes in Baroda, Rajkot, Bhavnagar and Ahmedabad charge Rs.125-150 per hour, often with coffee or snacks thrown in. If making a long call, it is possible to subscribe to a mobile phone. Airmail is a cheap way of communication, but can take between one and three weeks. The speed-post facility is better – there is a guarantee of delivery within a stipulated time, and you can ask for a proof of delivery receipt if you are making a long enough stay in the same city. Post offices at tourist destinations have special franks – you can ask for the Sidi syaid mosque cancellation mark at Ahmedabad GPO (General Post Office), the Indus valley cancellation mark at Lothal near Utelia, the Lion cancellation mark at Sasan-Gir near Junagadh, and so on. Picture postcards of tourist destinations are published by Gujarat Tourism, Archeological Survey of India, and by private entrepreneurs. Some Heritage Hotels, like the Gondal palace and Balaram palace, have their own picture postcards depicting their own property. High quality greetings cards can be purchased in the larger cities. Well known brands include Archies, and Feelings, and you can encourage worthy causes by buying cards from the local chapters of UNICEF, Child Relief and You, World Wide Fund for Nature, Beauty Without Cruelty and several more.

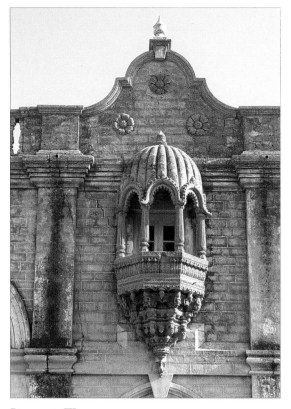

JAROKHA, WANKANER

WEIGHTS AND MEASURES

Gujarat adheres strictly to the decimal system. Distances are measured in kilometres, weights in grams and kilograms. The state has stringent laws regarding weights and measures.

WHAT ELSE TO SEE

Besides the royal palaces, mansions and forts, Gujarat has much to offer by way of sightseeing. The Indus valley civilisation thrived in this region from 2500-1500BC and its remains at Lothal, off the Ahmedabad-Bhavnagar highway, and at Dhoravira, in the Kutch district, have been developed for tourists. Mauryan relics can be seen at Junagadh, including 3rd century BC inscriptions of Emperor Ashoka, and 1st-5th centuries AD Buddhist caves. Beautiful Hindu temples, some of them now in ruins, but with fabulous examples of 8th-13th centuries AD sculpture still visible, include the Modhera sun temple and Shamlaji temple in northern Gujarat; Ghumli, Gop and Bileshwar temples near Porbandar; and Kera and Kotai temples in the Kutch district. Typical of Gujarat are the Jain and Hindu temple sites, spectacularly situated on high mountain peaks – the cluster of over 800 11th-19th centuries AD Jain temples, with their massed towers and marble sculpture at Shetrunjaya, on the hill overlooking Palitana, is Gujarat's major tourist draw. Equally impressive is the 12th century AD Jain temple cluster on Mount Girnar, 3,660 feet above sea level, and offering some splendid carvings and architecture; so too the 12th century AD Jain temples of Taranga, set in rocky mountains; and the 1062-1134AD carved marble Jain temples of Kumbharia in the Aravalis foothills.

Mosques and Islamic mausolea were built in the medieval period, and a Hindu element was added to the Islamic geometry in the 14th-16th centuries AD. The finest of these mosques, erected in the Indo-Saracenic style, can be seen at Ahmedabad, Champaner, Dholka and Cambay. Stepwells are considered an endemic architectural feature of Gujarat, though similar stepwells are also found in Rajasthan and Madya Pradesh. The 11th century AD stepwell at Patan, with seven flights of steps leading down to the water level, stringcoursed by exquisite sculpture, and culminating in chambers where it is believed royals came to enjoy the natural air conditioning effect of breezes wafting off the water; the late-15th century AD stepwell, also at Patan, with splendid carvings all the way down to the water; the stepwells of Wadhwan, and the massive stepwell of Ghumli, near Porbandar, are the best examples of this architectural style, evolved to combat the low groundwater level in these arid lands and to provide shelter for caravan travellers on warm afternoons in Gujarat.

The 1,660 kilometre coastline of Gujarat has its own sets of treasures. Fine beaches, with good swimming and water-sport facilities, can be found at Mandvi in Kutch, on the island of Diu, at Ahmedpur-Mandvi, near Diu, and in south eastern Gujarat. Chorwad, near Porbandar, and Gopnath, near Bhavnagar, are extremely scenic. Shore temples of considerable importance attract pilgrims and tourists to Somnath and Dwarka in Saurashtra, and to Narayan Sarovar-Koteshwar in Kutch. The colourful dockyards of Veraval and Porbandar, where dhows are made using traditional tools and hereditary skills, the lock-gated dock in Bhavnagar, the ship-breaking yards of Alang: these are all spectacular sights, and visitors really should not miss them.

Glossary of Terms

Clans and Dynasties

AGNIVANSHI Dynasties believed to have risen from the holy fire.

BABI A Muslim dynasty of Afghan origin, earlier subhedars of the Mughal empire in Gujarat, later established their own states at Balasinore, Junagadh (q.v.) and Radhanpur.

CHAUHAN A Rajput clan, claims to have risen from the holy fire. The Chauhans of Devgadh Baria, Chotta Udaipur (q.v.) etc in Gujarat are the Kheechi branch of the Chauhan clan.

GAEKWAD/GAEKWAR A Maratha dynasty, originally members of the armies of the Peshwas who rose as a major power on the ruins of the Mughal empire, but carved out independent kingdom at Baroda, which became one of the three most important princely states of India.

GOHIL A Rajput clan probably originating from the rulers of Mewar, but with early references in their history to Luni in Marwar; moved to Saurashtra in 12th century AD and established a capital at Gogha in 13th century AD. Founded states of Bhavnagar (q.v.), Palitana and Vallabhipur, and a member of the clan inherited Rajpipla (q.v.).

JADEJA/JAREJA A Rajput clan, claims descent from Lord Krishna, some believe them to be descendants of the army of Alexander the Great, came to Kutch (q.v.) from Sindh and later moved to Saurashtra (Kathiawad). See also Gondal, Jamnagar, Morvi and Rajkot.

JETHWA An ancient Rajput clan of Saurashtra. See Porbandar.

JHALA MAKWANA A Rajput clan from the Sindh-Baluchistan region, settled in Patdi, moved capital to Halwad and finally established its seat of power at Dhrangadhra (q.v.). See also Limbdi, Wadhwan and Wankaner.

KATHI/CATTI An important clan of Kutch and Saurashtra in the 12th century AD, believed to be of Scythic descent, very war like tribe, created problems for the more powerful Rajputs of Porbandar, Bhavnagar, Nawanagar etc by their courage, prominent in the hinterland of the Kathiawadi peninsula (Saurashtra) ruling from Babra, Jetpur, Jasdan (q.v.) etc. The Valas, Khacchers etc belong to this clan.

KHAMBATT A Muslim clan, went on to rule Cambay.

KRISHNAVANSHI Dynasties claiming lineage to Lord Krishna/moon god.

LOHANI A Muslim dynasty that originates from Lohan in Afghanistan. See Palanpur.

SOLANKI/VAGHELA An ancient Rajput clan, well known as the Chalukyas, which was a dominant ruling dynasty in Gujarat during the 10th-13th centuries AD, the golden period for Rajput architecture in Gujarat. Ruled mainly non-salute states and jagirs during British times in Gujarat, but were prominent in central India.

SURYAVANSHI Dynasties that claim descent from the sun god.

Titles

BAISA Female member of a ruling family.

BAPA/BAPU A male member of the ruling family (literally father) in Gujarat. In other states, like Rajasthan, it is Banna (Rajasthani for elder brother).

BEGUM Wife of a nawab.

DARBAR SAHEB Ruler, chieftain; also relatives of same.

DESAI Revenue collectors of any community. The Patels of Patdi were Desais, but became rulers of Patdi.

Glossary

DIWAN Minister.

HIS HIGHNESS/HH The ruler of a princely state.

JAGIRDAR Ruler of a jagir.

JAMINDAR Landed gentry with large estates but no real ruling power.

KUMAR/KUAR Heir to a jagir, younger sons of the ruler of a large state.

KUWARANI Wife of a kumar/kuar.

MAHARAJ KUMAR Second son of the maharajah.

MAHARAJAH/RAJA The title of the Hindu king of a major state.

MAHARAJAH SAHEB King.

MAHARANI Queen, wife of a maharana, maharajah or maharao.

MAHARANA/RANA The title of the ruler of Mewar, but conferred by him on rulers of some other clans which gave him assistance eg. the Jhala ruler of Dhrangadhra.

MAHARAO/RAO Another important Hindu title.

MALEK Muslim rulers of smaller states or jagirs eg. Dasada, Zainabad etc.

NAWAB Title given to a Muslim ruler of a major state.

NAWABZADI Daughter of a nawab.

RAJMATA Widow of a maharajah.

RANI SAHEBA/BEGUM SAHEBA Queen.

SUBHEDAR Governor, viceroy of Mughal court.

THAKORE SAHEB/THAKUR SAHEB Ruler of a small state or jagir.

THANEDAR Chief.

YUVRAJ Crown prince, heir apparent.

YUVRANI Wife of a crown prince.

NOTE Titles were up-graded with time eg. the Maleks of Palanpur became Nawabs of Palanpur, thakore sahebs became maharajahs etc. Titles are now abolished in India by law but still in common usage.

Architectural Periods

ART DECO Architecture, furniture and figurines of the 1930-40s AD in Europe, became a status symbol in India. See Morvi, Porbandar, Wankaner etc.

ART NOUVEAU Edwardian style of furniture and decoration.

BAROQUE An elaborate architectural style, based on the ancient classical architecture of Greece and Italy, that grew in popularity during the Renaissance in the 16th and 17th centuries AD in Europe. Style adopted heavily in Kathiawad and mainland Gujarat for example in Nawanagar (Jamnagar), Dhrangadhra etc.

CLASSICAL Ancient architecture of Greece and Italy, a style that revived during the Renaissance.

GOTHIC The kind of architecture that thrived in 13th-16th centuries AD Britain and in Europe, distinguished by its pointed arches and doors.

INDO-SARACENIC A blend of Hindu and Muslim architectural styles.

MUGHAL An Indo-Saracenic style using domed pavilions and geometrically laid out gardens with rectangular pools fed by fountains and well defined beds for flowers and shrubs.

REGENCY 19th century AD architecture during the Georgian period, introduced in Limbdi.

ROMANESQUE Architecture of 12th century AD Italy. See Rajpipla.

VENETIAN-GOTHIC Mediterranean style of Gothic architecture. Became very popular in Kathiawad eg. palaces of Gondal, Wankaner, Morvi, Junagadh etc.

Architectural Terms

ARABESQUE Decoration with intricate entertaining of leaves, scrollwork etc.

AINA MAHAL/SHEESH MAHAL Hall decorated with mirrors, glass or mirror/glass mosaics.

BALUSTER A row of intricate pillars supporting a rail.

BALUSTRADE Rail with set of balusters.

BASTION Semi-circular (sometimes angular) projection to strengthen a fort wall.

Glossary

BIRADARI Pavilion, sitting area.

BURJ Bastion, turreted watch tower.

BURMESE TEAK Teak wood from Burma.

CHATTRI/CHATTARDI Literally meaning umbrella, refers to domed structures, especially the royal cenotaphs which were dominated by domes, umbrella-like domed pavilions etc.

CHOWK Courtyard.

CUPOLA Small dome.

DARBARGADH A fortified palace complex of a ruler in a village, town or city. In earlier times, always contained the royal palace, administrative offices etc, but in later years rulers of larger states moved to new palaces in the suburbs and used darbargadhs only for administration.

DARBARHALL Hall for public and private audiences, official functions and celebrations.

GADH/KILLA A fort, usually a hill fort.

HAVELI From a Persian term, traditional mansions built around courtyards, known for their carvings of wood or stone, in later years influenced by European styles. Usually refers to the mansions of rich merchant communities, rulers of petty states or jagirs, diwans, desais, Naggar Brahmin/Shiya Muslim administrators etc.

IONIC Flowing capitals on a classical pillar.

JALI Literally a web or net, jalis in palaces and other buildings refer to traceries of perforation on stone and wood, or in some cases trellis-work on

metal. Generally latticed screens offering privacy to the royal family, but allowing light and breezes to enter the palaces.

JAROKHA Balcony/gallery of wood or stone, usually with intricate brackets and canopies.

KHUMBA Pillars.

KUND Stepped tank.

KUVA Cylindrical/square wells.

MANDIR Temple.

MAQBARA Muslim mausoleum.

MASJID Mosque.

MINARA Minarets.

NICHE Recess in wall for decorations.

NIWAS Residence.

POL Fortified gateway, little streets in walled city.

RANGAMANDAPA Painted hall, usually for marriages or ceremonies.

RAJMAHAL/HUZOOR BUNGALOW A royal palace.

SABHA MANDAPA Columned meeting place of a temple, preceding the sanctuary.

SHIKARA Curved and pointed towering roof of a temple.

STAMBHA Towers, minarets.

TORANA Intricate arches or projections on the

gate, usually supported by towers.

TURRET A watch tower.

YUVRAJ BUNGALOW The residence of the crown prince.

VAV Well with steps leading to the water level, often with galleries where royalty could enjoy breezes from over the water, landings for caravans to relax in the cool. Covered to protect the water.

VILAS Pleasure palace.

ZANANA A wing of the palace reserved for women, segregated women's apartments.

Objects

BUGGY/VICTORIA Horse drawn carriage.

BURQA Veil worn by Muslim women.

CASKET Ornate containers of gold or silver that carried messages or gifts for a ruler, usually from another princely state, on ceremonial occasions like coronations, anniversaries, birthdays etc.

CHAKRA Wheel.

GADI/ASANA Throne.

HOOKAH Water cooled smoking pipe.

HOWDAH Canopied seat on an elephant.

MANDAP Platform for a throne or ceremonial occasions.

PALANQUIN/DOLI Litter seat for one or more,

Glossary

usually held up by four men.

PATARA/MAJOOS Chests.

PUNKAH Fan.

SINHASAN Throne.

TIJORI Safe.

Geographic Terms

BEYT/BET Island, mounds of land in a desert.

DUNGAR/PAHAD Hills, mountains.

GOHILWAD Land of the Gohils, comprising the states of Bhavnagar, Palitana and Vallabhipur.

GUJARAT In history, the entire strip of land from the foothills of the Aravalis range before Rajasthan to the start of the Sahyadri range in the Dangs region, but now a state including Saurashtra and Kutch.

KATHIAWAD The peninsula enclosed by the western coast of the Arabian sea, Gulf of Cambay and Gulf of Kutch.

KUTCH The region between the Gulf of Kutch and the desert of Sindh – western Rajasthan, east towards the Aravalis range.

NADI River.

RANN Flat, saline desert plains (eg. Rann of Kutch), also battlefield.

SAROVAR Sea, also large lake or reservoir.

SAURASHTRA A term for the Kathiawadi peninsula.

TALAO Lake, tank.

TEKRA Hillock.

ZALAWAD The region ruled by Jhalas (states of Dhrangadhra, Surendranagar, Wadhwan, Wankaner etc).

General Terms

ACHARYA Traditional teacher.

AGNI Fire, usually in vedic terms.

ATCHA OK.

BADA-KHANA Major meal, usually ceremonial.

BHAGWAD GITA/UPANISHADS/VEDAS Hindu religious works.

BIRYANI Fragrant long staple rice, layered with herbs, browned onions, saffron and spices, with a choice of nuts and fruit, vegetables, mutton or chicken.

CHAUTH A fraction of income of the state given to a senior ruler: eg. the Maharajah of Baroda and Nawab of Junagadh extracted chauth from other rulers of Gujarat and Saurashtra respectively until the Walker Settlement of 1807AD.

DARBAR Early ruler or royal gathering.

DAWA Medicine.

DIWALI Leading Indian festival.

DUDHPUTTI Female infanticide by drowning in milk, prevalent in some Rajput and Patel communities.

JAGIR/TALUKDARI A petty state, whose rulers had limited powers eg. some jagirdars could not impose death sentences.

JAUHAR Self immolation by Rajput women when defeat of husbands' army was inevitable, as death was preferable to dishonour in Rajput tradition.

KADI A soup made from homemade curds.

KHALSA Merging a small state into an empire.

KHANA/BHOJAN Meal.

MOTOR GADDI Car.

NAAN Cornflour bread.

NASTA Snacks.

NAVRAT Colourful nine-night Indian festival.

NAZRANA Tribute offered to a more powerful ruler as a compromise during battle.

PANEER Homemade curdy cheese.

PRIVY PURSE Royal pension fixed for the rulers of princely states as compensation for loss of power and property, abolished in 1970s AD.

PULAOS Rice cooked with herbs, spices and vegetables.

PURDAH The custom of covering the face followed by Muslims and by Hindu royals. Often epitomised the conservative attitude of royal families towards their women.

Glossary

RAJ Rule.

RAJWADA/RAJWADI Princely state.

RAMAYANA/RAMLILA/MAHABHARATA/ PRAVIN SAGAR Great Hindu epics.

ROTIS Bread made from millet and wheat.

SALOON The royal railway carriage of the maharajahs and nawabs, generally suites of drawing, dining, bedroom, kitchen, bathroom and staff quarters!

SATI Self immolation on the funeral pyre of the husband.

SATYAGRAHA Passive resistance.

TILAK Mark made on the forehead.Rajtilak on king during coronation.

VAYU/PAWAN Wind.

YAGNA Ceremonial sacrifice.

Words of Greeting

JAI JINENDRA Greeting between Jains.

JAI MATA JI/JAI AMBE Greeting between followers of the Hindu goddesses.

JAI SHRI KRISHNA Good bye, among Hindus.

KHAMANGINI A greeting between Rajputs.

NAMASTE The commonest way of greeting in India, with hands folded.

SALAAM MALIEKUM Muslim greeting.

Bibliography

Allen, C. & Dwivedi, S.
Lives of the Indian Princes, Century Publishing, 1984
Allen, C.
Plain Tales from the Raj, Century in association with
André Deutsch Ltd & BBC, 1985
Basham, A. L.
The Wonder that was India, London, 1954
Batley, C.
Indian Architecture, London, 1934
Bhaitacharya, Sachidananda
A Dictionary of Indian History, George Braziller,
New York, 1967
Brown, H. ed.
The Sahibs, William Hodge & Co., Ltd., London, 1948
Caine, W. S.
Picturesque India, Routledge, 1898
Collins, L. & La Pierre, D.
Freedom at Midnight, Granada Publishing Ltd, 1982
Coomaraswamy, A. K.
Early India Architecture: Palaces, repr. Delhi, 1975
Crooke, W. (trans.)
Travels in India by Jean-Baptise Tavernier, London, 1925
Davies, P.
*The Penguin Guide to the Monuments of India, II, Islamic,
Rajput, European*, London, 1989
Desai, M.
Architektur in Gujarat, Indien, Zurich, 1990
Edwardes, M.
The Last Years of British India, Cassell, London, 1963
Edwardes, M.
Indian Temples and Palaces, London, 1970
Fabb, J.
Royal Tours of the British Empire 1860-1927,
BT Batsford, 1989
Fitze, Sir K.
Twilight of the Maharajas, John Murray, London, 1956
Fuller, C. J.
'Rituals of Kingship', in *The Camphor Flame: Popular
Hinduism and Society in India*, Princeton, 1992
Gaekwad, F. & Fass, V.
The Palaces of India, London, 1980
Gascoigne, B.
The Great Moguls, Time Books International, New Delhi, 1987
Ghurye, G. S.
Rajput Architecture, Bombay, 1968
Gonda, J.
Ancient Indian Kingship from the Religious Point of View,
Leiden, 1966
Goodall, Sir D.
Remembering India, Scorpion Cavendish, London, 1997
Gross, J.
Rudyard Kipling – The Man, His Work and His World,

Weidenfeld & Nicolson, London, 1972
Havell, E. B.
Indian Architecture, London, 1927
Hutton, J. H.
Caste in India – Its Nature, Function and Origins,
Cambridge University Press, 1946
Kumar, C. & Puri, M.
Mahatma Gandhi, His Life and Influence,
W. Heinemann, London, 1982
Lord, J.
The Maharajas, Hutchinson & Co., London, 1972
Lothian, A. C.
Kingdoms of Yesterday, John Murray, London, 1951
Mayer, A. C.
'Rulership and Divinity: the case of the modern Hindu
prince', *Modern Asian Studies*, 25/4 (1991)
Mayo, K.
Mother India, Jonathan Cape Ltd, 1927
Menon, V. P.
The Transfer of Power in India, Princeton, 1957
Metcalf, T. R.
An Imperial Vision: Indian Architecture and Britain's Raj,
London, 1989
Michell, G. & Martinelli, A.
The Royal Palaces of India, Thames & Hudson Ltd, 1994
Moorhouse, G.
India Britannica, William Collins & Sons & Co Ltd, 1983
Munshi, K. M.
End of an Era: Hyderabad Memories, Bharatiya Vidya
Bhavan, Bombay, 1957
Nanda, B. R.
Mahatma Gandhi – A Biography, George Allen & Unwin,
London, 1965
Nehru, J.
An Autobiography, Allied Publishers, New Delhi, 1962
Nicholson, L.
India Companion, Headline Book Publishing, 1996
Piggott, S
Some Ancient Cities of India, Oxford, 1945
Prasad, R. C.
Early English Travellers in India, Delhi, 1980
Ramusack, B.
The Princes of India in the Twilight of Empire,
Wiesbaden, 1980
Rao, Shiva B.
India's Freedom Movement, Orient Longmans, New Delhi, 1972
Robinson, A.
Maharaja: the Spectacular Heritage of Princely India,
New York and London, 1988
Roe, Sir T.
The Embassy of Sir Thomas Roe to India, 1615-19,
ed. W. Foster, London, 1926

Shankardass, R. D.
*Vallabhbhai Patel, Power & Organization in Indian
Politics*, Sangam Books Ltd, 1988
Sinhjee, Bhagvat
The Maker of Modern Gondal, Kevalchand Kanjibhai, Gondal, 1934
Sinhjee, Virbhadra
The Rajputs of Saurashtra, Popular Prakashan Pvt. Ltd,
Bombay, 1994
Slesin, S. & Cliff, S.
Indian Style, London, 1990
Spear, P.
A History of India, Penguin Books, London, 1970
Stocqueller, J. H.
The Hand Book of British India, W. M. H. Allen & Co.,
London, 1854
Tadgell, C.
The History of Architecture in India, London, 1990
Terraine, J.
The Life and Times of Lord Mountbatten, Arron Books,
London, 1970
Tilloston, S.
Indian Mansions, A Social History of the Haveli,
The Oleander Press, 1994
Tillotson, G. H. R.
The Rajput Palaces, New Haven, Conn. & London, 1987
Tod, Colonel J.
Annals and Antiquities of Rajasthan, Smith Elder & Co.,
London, 1829
Toy, S.
Strongholds of India, London, 1957
Trevelyan, H.
The India We Left, Macmillan, London, 1972
Vadgama, K.
India in Britain, Robert Royce Ltd, 1984
Ward, P.
Gujarat, Daman, Diu, The Oleander Press, 1994
Watson, F.
India, A Concise History, Thames & Hudson, 1974
Welch, S. C. & Patnaik, N.
A Second Paradise: Indian Courtly Life 1590-1947,
New York, 1985
Wheeler, M. ed.
*Splendours of the East: Temples, Tombs, Palaces and
Fortresses of Asia*, London, 1965
Woodruff, P.
*The Men Who Ruled India (Vol. I, The Founders; Vol. II,
The Guardians)*, Jonathan Cape, London, 1954
Woodward, W. H.
Extracts from an Outline of the British Empire 1500-1932AD,
Cambridge University Press, 1932
Worswick, C.
Princely India, Hamish Hamilton, 1980

Personae

Personae

Sardar Rao Bahudar Bechardas
   Viharidas Desai
Sher Khan Babi
Sir J B Peile
Sultan Muhammad Bhegada
Zulficar

KUTCH   66-71
Alexander the Great
Colonel Wilkinson
Emperor Jehangir
Jadejas, The
Maharao Desalji
Maharao Godji
Maharao Khegarji the third
Maharao Khengarji
Maharao Lakhpat Sinh
Maharao Madan Sinhji
Maharao Pragmalji
Ram Singh

LIMBDI   72-73
Harpaldeo Sinh
Jhalas, The
Mangoji
Thakore Saheb Chatrashailya Sinh
Thakore Saheb Rana Sir Jaswant
   Sinhji

MORVI   74-77
Aloiji
Draupati
HH Maharajah Lakdhir Sinhji
HH Maharajah Mahendra Sinhji
HH Maharajah Waghji
Jadejas, The
Leah
Maharani Vijaykuverba
Manibai
Mayur
Meru Khwas
Pragmalji
Purna
Rangji (Ravaji)
Raukhsmani
Thakore Saheb Hamirji
Thakore Saheb Jiaji
Thakore Saheb Kavoji
Thakore Saheb Ravaji the second
Uma
Vishal

PALANPUR   78-83
Begum Jahanara
Diwan Firoz Khan Lohani
Emperor Akhbar
Emperor Jehangir
HH Maharajah Ganga Sinhji
HH Nawab Saheb Joravar Khan
HH Nawab Saheb Sher Khan Babi
HH Nawab Saheb Sir Taley
   Muhammad Khan
HH Nawab Saheb Zorawar Khan
Kanji Koli
King George VI
Lohanis, The
Lohanis of Jalore
Lord Mountbatten
Malek Khuram Khan
Malek Yusuf Khan
Nawab Iqbal Muhammad Khan
   Lohani
Pahad Khan Lohani
Palandeo Sinh
Pathans, The
Solanki Rajput kings
Sultan All-a-ud-din Khilji
Trimmanna Solanki
Vishaldev Sinh

PATDI   84-86
Dilip Sinhji Desai Patel
Gandhi
Jhalas, The
Jhaverbhai Patel
Nehru
Shantilal Parbhoodas Patel
Sultan Ahmed Shah
Vallabhbhai Patel

PORBANDAR   87-93
Anant Kunverba
Ayesha de Silva
Bactrian Greeks, The
Halaman
HH Maharana Bhav Sinhji
HH Maharana Harendra
   de Silva QC
HH Maharana Natwarsinhji
Jadejas, The
Jetha
Jethwa
Jethwas, The

Jyeshthamitra Shung
Karamchand Gandhi
Maharana Sartanji
Mahatma Gandhi
Mohandas Karamchand Gandhi
Nagarjoon
Nihal de Silva
Pushyamitrs Shung
Ravindranath Tagore
Rajmata Rupaliben
Santokben
Savji Parikh
Vasumitra
Yethas, The
Yuvraj Udaimansinhji

RAJKOT   94-95
Ajoji
Aurangzeb
Azam Khan
Bamanioji
Captain Ballantyne
HH Thakore Saheb Dharmendra
   Sinhji
HH Thakore Saheb Lakdiraj Sinhji
HH Thakore Saheb Lakhajiraj
   Sinhji
HH Thakore Saheb Prahlad Sinhji
Jawaharlal Nehru
Kanoji
Karamchand Gandhi
Karsandas
Kathis, The
Mahatma Gandhi
Maheramanaji
Masum Khan
Meramanaji
Meramanaji the fourth
Mota Kumbhaji
Ranmalji the second
Ravindranath Tagore
Sahebji
Shah Jahan
Thakore Saheb Manohar Sinhji
Vaghela Princess of Sardhar
Vaghelas, The
Vibhoji
Yuvraj Mandatta Sinh

RAJPIPLA   96-105
Arjun Sinhji

Bhils, The
Chokrana
Damaji Gaekwad
Emperor Akhbar
Emperor Aurangazeb
Gaekwads, The
Gemal Sinhji
Gohils, The
Hari Sinh
HH Maharajah Chattra Sinhji
HH Maharajah Kumar Indrajeet
   Sinhji
HH Maharajah Natwar Sinhji
HH Maharajah Raghuvir Sinhji
HH Maharajah Vijay Sinhji
Jeet Sinhji
King Mokhadaji
King Shivaji
Maharana Pratap
Maharana Udai Sinhji
Maharani Rukmani Devi
Marathas, The
Parmaras, The
Princess Mohini Kuar
Pritviraj Sinhji
Raja Gambhir Sinhji
Rani Hemlata Devi
Rao Saheb of Poshina
Samar Sinhji
Sultan Ahmed Shah
Sultan Muzzaffar Shah
Verisal
Verisal the second
Vijaypat
Yuvraj Manvendar Sinhji

WADHWAN   106-110
HH Maharajah Amar Sinhji
HH Maharajah Bane Sinhji
HH Maharajah Chaitanya Dev
   Sinhji
HH Maharajah Surendra Sinhji
HH Thakore Saheb Bal Sinhji
HH Thakore Saheb Dajiraj Sinhji
HH Thakore Saheb Jaswant Sinhji
HH Thakore Saheb Zoravar Sinhji
Jhalas, The
Mr Mayer
Princess of Vizakapatnam
Yuvraj Sidharth Sinhji

WANKANER   111-119
HH Jam Saheb Ranjit Sinhji
HH Maharajah Amar Sinhji
HH Maharajah Bane Sinhji
HH Maharajah Pratap Sinh
Jhalas, The
Karamchand Gandhi
Mahatma Gandhi
Prince Jehangir
Sardar Patel
Sartanji
Yuvraj Dr Digvijay Sinh
Yuvraj Ranjit Sinh

OTHER STATES
AND AREAS   120-123
Ahmed Kaji
Ahmed Malek
Amir Mustafa
Aurangzeb
Azam Khan
Baroboza
Chudasamas, The
Dom Constantino de Braganca
Dom Diogo de Noronha
Emperor Akhbar
Emperor Jehangir
Gaekwads, The
Ishak
Khwaja Safar
King James I
Kshatrapas, The
Mahatma Gandhi
Mahidas, The
Malek Ayaz
Marathas, The
Mauryan emperors, The
Mr Dunlop
Nuno da Cunha
Ramashah
Sardar Vallabhbhai Patel
Shah Jahan
Shaik Ahmed Ganj Baksh
Shiya Muslims, The
Sir Thomas Roe
Solanki Rajputs, The
Sulaiman Pasha
Sultan Ahmed Shah
Sultan Bahadur Shah
Tughan
Udadbir